BEC Higher

PRACTICE TESTS FROM THE UNIVERSITY OF CAMBRIDGE LOCAL EXAMINATIONS SYNDICATE

 CAMBRIDGE
UNIVERSITY PRESS

PUBLISHED BY THE PRESS SYNDICATE OF THE UNIVERSITY OF CAMBRIDGE
The Pitt Building, Trumpington Street, Cambridge, United Kingdom

CAMBRIDGE UNIVERSITY PRESS
The Edinburgh Building, Cambridge CB2 2RU, United Kingdom   http://www.cambridge.org
40 West 20th Street, New York, NY 10011–4211, USA
477 Williamstown Road, Port Melbourne, VIC 3207, Australia
Ruiz de Alarcón 13, 28014 Madrid, Spain
Dock House, The Waterfront, Cape Town 8001, South Africa

First published 2002

This is a new version of *Cambridge BEC3*, published in 2000, revised and updated to meet the
needs of the new BEC curriculum.

Typeset in Sabon 10.5/12pt and Univers 10/13pt   System 3b2   [CE]

Printed in the United Kingdom at the University Press, Cambridge

ISBN 0 521 752892 Book
ISBN 0 521 752906 Cassette
ISBN 0 521 752914 Audio CD

Contents

Thanks and acknowledgements

The authors and publishers are grateful to the following copyright owners for permission to reproduce copyright material. Every endeavour has been made to contact copyright holders and apologies are expressed for any omissions.

pp. 42 and 45 Letts Educational; p. 44 adapted from the article by Kim Thomas in *The Independent* 15.02.96; p. 60 from *Marketing Strategy* by Paul Fifield. Reprinted by permission of Butterworth Heinemann; pp. 62 and 80 by Neasa MacErlean, © *The Guardian*; p. 63 from 'Young Brits aim to conquer new peaks' by Edward Fennell Times International Newspapers Ltd, 22 February 1996; p. 73 from *Guide to Management Gurus* by Carol Kennedy published by Century Business 1991.

Introduction

TO THE STUDENT

This book is for candidates preparing for the University of Cambridge Local Examinations Syndicate (UCLES) Business English Certificate Higher Level examination. It contains four complete tests which have been updated to reflect the most recent specifications (introduced in March 2002).

The BEC Suite

The Business English Certificates (BEC) are certificated examinations which can be taken on up to six fixed dates per year at approved Cambridge BEC centres. They are aimed primarily at individual learners who wish to obtain a business-related English language qualification and provide an ideal focus for courses in Business English. Set in a business context, BEC tests English language, not business knowledge. BEC is available at three levels – Preliminary, Vantage and Higher.

BEC Higher

Within the three levels, BEC Higher is at Cambridge Level 4.

Cambridge Level 4 BEC Higher
Cambridge Level 3 BEC Vantage
Cambridge Level 2 BEC Preliminary

The exam is based on the former Business English Certificate 3, which has been revised to keep pace with changes in business practice and language teaching and testing, and renamed.

The BEC Higher examination consists of four papers:

Reading and Writing	1 hour
Writing	1 hour 10 minutes
Listening	40 minutes (approximately)
Speaking	16 minutes

Test of Reading

This paper consists of six parts with 52 questions, which take the form of two multiple matching tasks, two multiple choice tasks, a cloze test and an error identification task. Part 1 contains five short texts or a longer text divided into five sections, and Parts 2, 3, 4, 5 and 6 each contain one longer text. The texts are taken from newspapers, business magazines, business correspondence, books, leaflets, brochures, etc. They are all business related, and are selected to test a wide range of reading skills and strategies.

Test of Writing

For this paper, candidates are required to produce two pieces of Writing. For Part 1, they write a short report based on graphic input. For Part 2, they choose whether to write a piece of business correspondence, a short report or a proposal. Candidates are asked to write 120 to 140 words for Part 1 and 200 to 250 words for Part 2. Assessment is based on achievement of task, range and accuracy of vocabulary and grammatical structures, organisation, content and appropriacy of register and format.

Test of Listening

This paper consists of three parts with 30 questions, which take the form of a note completion task, a multiple matching task and a multiple choice task. Part 1 contains a monologue in a work-related situation, Part 2 contains five very short monologues, and Part 3 contains one longer conversation between two or more people. The texts are audio-recordings based on a variety of sources including interviews, face to face conversations and documentary features. They are all business related, and are selected to test a wide range of listening skills and strategies.

Test of Speaking

The Speaking Test consists of three parts, which take the form of an interview section, a short talk on a business topic, and a discussion. Candidates are examined in pairs by two examiners, an Interlocutor and an Assessor. The Assessor awards a mark based on the following criteria: Grammar and Vocabulary, Discourse Management, Pronunciation and Interactive Communication. The Interlocutor provides a global mark for the whole test.

Marks and results

The four BEC Higher papers total 120 marks, after weighting. Each paper is weighted to 30 marks. A candidate's overall grade is based on the total score gained in all four papers. It is not necessary to achieve a satisfactory level in all four papers in order to pass the examination. Pass grades are A, B or C, with A being the highest. D and E are failing grades. Every candidate is provided with a Statement of Results which includes a graphical display of their performance in each paper. These are shown against the scale Exceptional – Good – Borderline – Weak and indicate the candidate's relative performance in each paper.

TO THE TEACHER

Candidature

Each year BEC is taken by over 50,000 candidates throughout the world. Most candidates are either already in work or studying in preparation for the world of work.

Content, preparation and assessment .

Material used throughout BEC is as far as possible authentic and free of bias, and reflects the international flavour of the examination. The subject matter should not advantage or disadvantage certain groups of candidates, nor should it offend in areas such as religion, politics or sex.

TEST OF READING

PART	MAIN SKILL FOCUS	Input: Text type, content	Response:	No. of Items /marks
1	Reading for gist and global meaning	Authentic business-related text – either a single text of 5 short, related texts (about 450 words in total)	Matching	8
2	Reading for structure and detail	Authentic business-related text (450–500 words) with sentence-length gaps	Matching	6
3	Understanding general points and specific details	Longer text based on authentic source material (500–600 words)	4-option multiple choice	6
4	Reading – vocabulary and structure	Single business-related text with primarily lexical gaps (approx. 250 words)	4-option multiple choice cloze	10
5	Reading – structure and discourse features	Single business-related text with structure and discourse gaps (approx. 250 words)	Rational deletion Open cloze	10
6	Reading – understanding sentence structure; error identification	Short text (150–200 words) Identification of additional unnecessary words in text	Proof reading	12

Reading Part One

This is a matching task. The text is approximately 450 words long, and is made up of five related short texts of authentic origin. Examples could be a set of related product descriptions, a set of advertisements (for instance, for different types of services), notices or messages, book or video reviews, short newspaper items on related topics.

Texts may be edited, but the source is authentic. They are identified as texts A–E.

There are eight items, each of which is one sentence long, numbered 1–8. Each sentence is a statement which can be matched with only one of the texts. The candidate's task is to read the sentence and then scan the texts for the one to which the sentence applies. Candidates are tested on whether they can understand the language of the item and relate it to the meaning of the text, which is expressed in different language.

Preparation
- present students with sets of related short texts (e.g. job advertisements, hotels, etc.) from newspapers, magazines, brochures;
- longer texts may also be divided into sub-headed sections;
- students should be encouraged to identify facts or ideas within each text, describing how the texts are similar and what differences they contain;
- the register or style of the task sentences is likely to differ from that of the texts and students should be given practice in recognising the same information in different styles, e.g. by re-writing advertisements into objective prose;
- the task is designed to go beyond simple word-matching and students will need to practise paraphrasing;
- activities that help students to identify target information among otherwise superfluous text (e.g. choosing what to watch from TV listings) would be beneficial;
- above all, students should treat the task as an example of information-processing skills which are frequently employed in social and professional life.

Reading Part Two

This is a gapped text with six sentence-length gaps. The text is 450 to 500 words long, and comes from an authentic business-related source, although it may be edited. Sources include business articles from newspapers or magazines, books on topics such as management, or company literature such as annual reports. Candidates have to read the text and then identify the correct sentence to fill each gap from a set of eight sentences marked A–H. Sentence H is the example, and one other sentence is a distractor which does not fit any of the gaps. Understanding, not only of the meaning of the text but of some of the features of its structure, is tested.

Preparation
- this task requires an overt focus on cohesion and coherence to which many students may not be accustomed;
- it would be helpful for students to piece back together texts that have been cut up, discussing why texts fit together as they do;
- it would be useful for students also to discuss why sentences that do not fit together do not do so;
- students could benefit from altering the cohesion of texts to make sentences that do not fit together do so, and vice versa;
- since culture affects discourse, including the order of argument development, discussions exploring this would be beneficial;

- the cut and paste functions of word-processing, where available, could be exploited for this task.

Reading Part Three

This task consists of a text accompanied by four-option multiple choice items. The stem of a multiple choice item may take the form of a question or an incomplete sentence. There are six items, which are placed after the text. The text is 500 to 600 words long. Sources of original texts may be the general and business press, company literature and books on topics such as management. Texts may be edited, but the source is authentic.

Preparation
- multiple choice questions are a familiar and long-standing type of test; here they are used to test opinion and inference rather than straightforward facts;
- correct answers are not designed to depend on simple word-matching, and students' ability to interpret paraphrasing should be developed;
- students should be encouraged to pursue their own interpretation of relevant parts of the text and then check their idea against the options offered, rather than reading all the options first;
- it could be useful for students to be given perhaps one of the wrong options only, and for them to try to write the correct answer and another wrong option.

Reading Part Four

This task is a modified cloze: in other words, a gapped text in which the gaps are carefully chosen. There are ten multiple choice items, most of which test vocabulary.

The text is approximately 250 words long, and is based on authentic source material of one of the text types listed above. The candidate's task is to choose the correct option, from the four available, to fill each gap.

Preparation
- it is important for students to appreciate that the correct answer in each case is correct in relation to the gap itself, rather than in relation to the other three options;
- it is worth emphasising that this task tests lexical and collocational knowledge, and that the best route to this knowledge is to read widely within the kinds of texts that the task employs;
- it is worth discussing what aspects of linguistic knowledge are tested (collocations, fixed phrases, register, etc.);
- it might be useful to give students gapped texts and have them produce alternative words which fit and which do not fit the gaps;
- any vocabulary-building activity is likely to be helpful in preparing for this task.

Reading Part Five

This task is an open cloze: a gapped text in which the candidate has to supply the word to fill each gap. There are ten items. Gaps are formed by rational deletion, being chosen rather than being simply those which occur if (for example) every seventh word is deleted. The focus is on structure, and coherence/cohesion in the text. Items tested may include prepositions, auxiliary verbs, pronouns, conjunctions, etc.

The text is based on authentic material, and it is approximately 250 words long. A title is usually included.

Preparation
- the kinds of words which are gapped may well correspond to the kinds of errors students make and therefore discussion of photocopied examples of students' compositions could be helpful;
- students should be encouraged to circle the word or words in the text that dictate what the answer is, in order for them to see that such clues to the answer may be adjacent to the gap or several words distant;
- students should brainstorm various likely words which might fit a particular gap, and then discuss why the ones that do not fit do not do so;
- students could be given several possible answers for a gap and discuss why the correct answer is correct;
- this task tests grammatical and structural aspects of language and any practice in these areas should be beneficial.

Reading Part Six

This is an error-correction or proof-reading task based on a text of 150 to 200 words, with twelve items. Candidates identify additional or unnecessary words in a text.

This task can be related to the authentic task of checking a text for errors, and suitable text types are therefore letters, publicity materials, etc. The text is presented with twelve numbered lines, which are the lines containing the items. Further lines at the end may complete the text, but they are not numbered.

Preparation
- students should be reminded that this task represents a kind of editing that is common practice, even in their first language;
- any work on error analysis is likely to be helpful for this task;
- it may well be that photocopies of students' own writing could provide an authentic source for practice;
- a reverse of the exercise (giving students texts with missing words) might prove beneficial.

Marks

One mark is given for each correct answer. The total score is then weighted to 30 marks for the whole Reading paper.

TEST OF WRITING

PART	Functions/Communicative Task	Input	Response:	Register
1	e.g. describing or comparing figures from graphic input, making inferences	Rubric and graphic input	Short report (medium may be memo or email) (120–140 words)	Neutral/ informal
2	**Report**: describing, summarising **Proposal**: describing, summarising, recommending, persuading **Correspondence**: e.g. explaining, apologising, reassuring, complaining	Rubric, possibly supplemented by brief input text, e.g. notice, advert,	**Candidates choose from** report (medium could be memo or email) or proposal (medium could be memo or email) or business correspondence (medium may be letter, fax or email) (200–250 words)	Neutral/ formal

For BEC Higher, candidates are required to produce two pieces of Writing:
- a short report based on graphic input;
- one of the following (of the candidate's choosing):
  - a piece of business correspondence; this means correspondence with somebody outside the company (e.g. a customer or supplier) on a business-related matter, and the delivery medium may be a letter, fax or email;
  - a report; the report will contain an introduction, main body of findings and conclusion; it is possible that the report may be delivered through the medium of a memo or an email;
  - a proposal; this has a similar format to a report, but unlike the report, the focus of the proposal is on the future, with the main focus being on recommendations for discussion; it is possible that the proposal may be delivered through the medium of a memo or an email.

Writing Part One

This is a guided writing task, in which the candidate produces a brief (120–140 word) report. The task provides a realistic situation in which it is necessary to analyse some sort of graphic input and express the information it conveys in words. Graphs, bar charts and pie charts of the type frequently used in the business pages of newspapers, company reports and brochures may provide a starting point. The graphic input is taken from an authentic source, but may be modified in the same way that a text may be edited. The rubric acts to amplify and clarify the situation, as well as making clear what the task involves.

Writing Part Two

In most parts of the BEC Writing tests, all candidates are required to perform the same task because there is no danger of individuals or groups of candidates being disadvantaged by that task. The exception is BEC Higher Writing Part Two: in order to generate the range of language which is characteristic of this level of language learner, the task contains no input or minimal input, resulting in a relatively high background knowledge requirement from the candidate. In the absence of a choice of tasks this would be likely to disadvantage some candidates, so a choice of tasks is given.

Candidates choose from three options: a report, proposal or a piece of business correspondence. The task is supplied by the rubric, which provides an authentic reason for writing, and indicates who the piece of writing is being produced for. The input is therefore more detailed and specific than that of the traditional 'essay question' task type.

Preparing for the Writing questions

The first writing task involves the kind of graphic input of information which is common in the business world, and students should be exposed to a wide range of examples of graphs and charts from newspapers, magazines, company literature, etc. The interpretation involved is the translating of the graphic input into prose, rather than the recommending of action. Students should have practice in the clear and concise presentation of written information. Specific vocabulary and phrasing should also be developed.

The second writing task requires students to plan carefully in order to be able to produce successful answers. They should be given practice in considering:
- the target reader;
- the purpose of writing;
- the requirements of the format (letter, report, etc.);
- the main points to be addressed;
- the approximate number of words to be written for each point;
- suitable openings and closings;
- the level of formality required.

Exposure to, and discussion of, as wide a range as possible of relevant texts would be beneficial.

Assessment

An impression mark is awarded to each piece of writing using the general mark scheme. Examiners use band descriptors to assess language and task achievement. Each piece of writing is assigned to a band between 0 and 5 and can be awarded one of two performance levels within that Band. Acceptable performance at BEC Higher level is represented by a band 3.

The general impression mark scheme is used in conjunction with a task-specific mark scheme, which focuses on criteria specific to each particular task. This summarises the content, organisation, register, format and effect on target reader indicated in the task.

American spelling and usage is acceptable.

The Band scores awarded are translated to a mark out of 10 for Part 1 and a mark out of 20 for Part 2.

Band	
5	Full realisation of the task set. • All content points included. • Controlled, natural use of language; minimal errors. • Wide range of structure and vocabulary. • Effectively organised, with appropriate use of cohesive devices. • Register and format consistently appropriate. Very positive effect on the reader.
4	Good realisation of the task set. • All major content points included; possibly minor omissions. • Natural use of language; errors only when complex language is attempted. • Good range of structure and vocabulary. • Generally well-organised, with attention paid to cohesion. • Register and format on the whole appropriate. Positive effect on the reader.
3	Reasonable achievement of the task set. • All major content points included; possibly minor omissions. • Reasonable control, although a more ambitious attempt at the task may lead to a number of non-impeding errors. • Adequate range of structure and vocabulary. • Organisation and cohesion is satisfactory. • Register and format reasonable, although not entirely successful. Satisfactory effect on the reader.
2	Inadequate attempt at the task set. • Some major content points omitted or inadequately dealt with; possibly some irrelevance. • Errors sometimes obscure communication and are likely to be numerous. • Limited range of structure and vocabulary; language is too elementary for this level. • Content is not clearly organised. • Unsuccessful attempt at appropriate register and format. Negative effect on the reader.
1	Poor attempt at the task set. • Notable content omissions and / or considerable irrelevance. • Serious lack of control; frequent basic errors. • Narrow range of structure and vocabulary. • Lack of organisation. • Little attempt at appropriate register and format. Very negative effect on the reader.
0	Achieves nothing. Either fewer than 25% of the required number of words or totally illegible or totally irrelevant.

TEST OF LISTENING

PART	MAIN SKILL FOCUS	Input	Item type	No. of Items
1	Listening for and noting specific information	Informational monologue	Gap filling requiring limited written responses (i.e. no more than 3 words)	12
2	Listening to identifying topic, context, function speaker's opinion etc	5 short monologues linked by theme or topic, from 5 different speakers	Multiple matching	10
3	Listening for gist, specific information, attitudes etc	Conversation/interview/discussion between 2 or more people	3-option Multiple choice	8

Listening Part One

This is a sentence-completion, gap-filling or note-taking task. The candidate has to supply only the key words of the answer, which will not be more than three words per item.

The spoken text lasts about two to three minutes and is a monologue. The text is heard twice. It is informational, and focuses on a series of identifiable facts. Topics might involve instructions, changes in arrangements or instructions, the programme for an event or meeting of some kind or details of the organisation of an event. The setting for the task could be someone giving information over the telephone, or a speaker addressing a roomful of delegates at a conference or people on a training course.

Listening tasks may be based on recorded material taken from authentic sources or more usually on scripted material. There are twelve items, which are distributed evenly throughout the text, so that candidates have time to record their answers. Answers to items may be numbers or amounts of money, but these will not involve the candidate in any calculations. Items of information are tested in the same order in which the information occurs in the text.

Listening Part Two

This is a matching task based on five short extracts linked by theme or topic and spoken by five different speakers, in monologue form. The texts last a total of approximately three to four minutes.

There are two tasks for each of the five extracts. These tasks relate to the content and purpose of the extracts, and candidates are asked to do any combination of the following: identify speakers, interpret context, recognise the function of what is said, identify the topic, understand specific information, identify a speaker's opinion or feelings.

The series of extracts is heard twice, and candidates must attempt both tasks during this time. It is for the candidates to decide whether they choose to do the first task the first time they listen to the text, and the second task the second time, or whether to deal with the two tasks for each extract together. For each task, they have a list of eight options to choose from.

Materials for this task are scripted, and relate to a business topic or situation.

Listening Part Three

This task consists of a dialogue usually with two or more speakers. There are eight items, which are three-option multiple choice. The task relates to a topic of interest or concern in the world of work. The text is heard twice.

Preparing for the Listening Paper

All listening practice should be helpful for students, whether authentic or specially prepared. In particular, discussion should focus on:
- the purpose of speeches and conversations or discussions;
- the roles of speakers;
- the opinions expressed;
- the language functions employed;
- relevant aspects of phonology such as stress, linking and weak forms, etc.

In addition, students should be encouraged to appreciate the differing demands of each task type. It will be helpful not only to practise the task types in order to develop a sense of familiarity and confidence, but also to discuss how the three task types relate to real life skills and situations:
- the first is note-taking (and therefore productive), and students should reflect on the various situations in which they take notes from a spoken input. They should also be encouraged to try to predict the kinds of words or numbers that might go in the gaps;
- the second is a matching (with discrimination) exercise, and reflects the ability to interrelate information between reading and listening and across differing styles and registers;
- the third involves the correct interpretation of spoken input, with correct answers often being delivered across different speakers.

In all three tasks, successful listening depends on correct reading, and students should be encouraged to make full use of the pauses during the test to check the written input.

Marks

One mark is given for each correct answer, giving a total score of 30 marks for the whole Listening paper.

TEST OF SPEAKING

PART	MAIN FOCUS	TIME	CANDIDATE FOCUS
1	Conversation between the interlocutor and each candidate. Giving personal information. Talking about present circumstances, past experiences and future plans, expressing opinions, speculating etc.	About 3 minutes	The interlocutor encourages the candidates to give information about themselves and to express personal opinions.
2	A 'mini presentation' by each candidate on a business theme. Organising a larger unit of discourse. Giving information and expressing opinions.	About 6 minutes	The candidates are given prompts which generate a short talk on a business-related topic.
3	Two-way conversation between candidates followed by further prompting from the interlocutor. Expressing and justifying opinions, speculating, comparing and contrasting, agreeing and disagreeing etc.	About 7 minutes	The candidates are presented with a discussion on a business-related topic. The interlocutor extends the discussion with further spoken prompts.

The Speaking Test is conducted by two Oral Examiners (an Interlocutor and an Assessor), with pairs of candidates. The Interlocutor is responsible for conducting the Speaking Test and is also required to give a mark for each candidate's performance during the whole test. The Assessor is responsible for providing an analytical assessment of each candidate's performance and, after being introduced by the Interlocutor, takes no further part in the interaction.

The Speaking Test is designed for pairs of candidates. However, where a centre has an uneven number of candidates, the last three candidates will be examined together. Oral Examiner packs contain shared tasks which are particularly appropriate for these groups of three.

Speaking Part One

For this part of the test, the Interlocutor asks the candidates questions on a number of personal or work-related subjects.

Speaking Part Two

In this part, each candidate's task is to choose one topic from a set of three, and to talk on it for one minute. Candidates have one minute in which to prepare, and should use this time to make brief notes. The other candidate listens and is invited to ask one or two questions at the end of each talk. The candidate may also make notes while listening to their partner. Each candidate is given a different set of three tasks from which to choose.

Candidates are again advised to keep in mind the business orientation of this test. It is wise to structure the one-minute talk, for example, as points, with an introduction and conclusion (however brief these must, of necessity, be) and to make the structure explicit when giving the talk, in order to show some evidence of planning. Candidates should approach the task as if giving a presentation in a business environment.

Examples of topic areas for the individual speaking task include the following: advertising, career planning, communications, customer relations, finance, health and safety, management (personnel, production, transport, etc.), marketing, recruitment, sales, technology, training and travel.

Speaking Part Three

This is a two-way collaborative task based on a prompt which is given to both candidates. The prompt consists of several sentences stating a business-related situation followed by two discussion points. Candidates are given time to read the prompt and then they discuss the situation together.

Examiners will be looking for a serious, adult approach to the discussion of the task, with the type of interaction which would be appropriate to a work environment. Candidates need to approach the task as a simulation, imagining themselves in a work environment, faced with a real situation to discuss and on which they should try to reach some decisions. The opinions they express, however, are their own. They are not instructed, as in some kinds of role play, to assume particular attitudes or opinions.

Preparing for the Speaking test

Students should be made familiar with the seating arrangements and paired assessment procedures that the Speaking test employs. Any speaking practice should be of benefit, in particular paired and small group work.

- For **Part One**, students should be familiar with the topics that the test covers, and that they should therefore be ready to deal with. Activities designed to develop fluency will be of considerable benefit, as the students need to demonstrate as wide a range of language as possible within the time limits of the test. It should be noted that not only is the test designed to minimise the possibility of attempts to use rehearsed speech, but also that examiners will quickly identify it.
- For **Part Two**, they need to develop the ability to prepare effectively for the long turn they are required to take. They should be given help in developing the skill of long-turn-taking, and in building up a range of discourse features to make their speech both coherent and cohesive. It is also important for them to listen to the other candidate, and be ready to ask relevant questions.
- For **Part Three**, candidates will benefit from practice in this kind of simulation, where they have to put themselves into a work environment, and collaborate to discuss and decide issues. They should be helped to build up a range of resources for turn-taking and the general negotiating of ideas and opinions.

Assessment

Candidates are assessed on their own performance and not in relation to each other according to the following analytical criteria; Grammar and Vocabulary, Discourse Management, Pronunciation and Interactive Communication. These criteria are interpreted at Higher level. Assessment is based on performance in the whole test.

Both examiners assess the candidates. The Assessor applies detailed, analytical scales, and the Interlocutor applies a Global Achievement Scale which is based on the analytical scale.

Grammar and Vocabulary

This refers to range and accuracy as well as the appropriate use of grammatical and lexical forms. At BEC Higher level a range of grammar and vocabulary is needed to deal with the tasks. At this level grammar is mainly accurate and vocabulary is used effectively.

Discourse Management

This refers to the coherence, extent and relevance of each candidate's individual performance. Contributions should be adequate to deal with the BEC Higher level tasks. Candidates should produce utterances which are appropriate in length.

Pronunciation

This refers to the candidates' ability to produce comprehensible utterances. At BEC Higher level, meanings are conveyed through the appropriate use of stress, rhythm, intonation and clear individual sounds, although there may be occasional difficulty for the listener.

Interactive Communication

This refers to the candidate's ability to take an active part in the development of the discourse. At BEC Higher level, candidates should be sensitive to turn taking throughout most of the test and hesitation should not demand patience of the listener.

Global Achievement Scale

This refers to the candidate's overall performance throughout the test.

Throughout the Speaking Test candidates are assessed on their language skills and in order to be able to make a fair and accurate assessment of each candidate's performance, the examiners must be given an adequate sample of language to assess. Candidates must, therefore, be prepared to provide full answers to the questions asked by either the Interlocutor or the other candidate, and to speak clearly and audibly. While it is the responsibility of the Interlocutor, where necessary, to manage or direct the interaction, thus ensuring that both candidates are given an equal opportunity to speak, it is the responsibility of the candidates to maintain the interaction as much as possible.

Candidates who take equal turns in the interchange will utilise to best effect the amount of time available.

Grading and results

Grading takes place once all scripts have been returned to UCLES and marking is complete. This is approximately five weeks after the examination. There are two main stages: grading and awards.

Grading

The four papers total 120 marks, after weighting. Each paper represents 25% of the total marks available.

The overall grade boundaries (A, B, C, D and E) are set using the following information:

- statistics on the candidature
- statistics on the overall candidate performance
- statistics on individual items, for those parts of the examination for which this is appropriate (Reading and Listening).
- the advice of the Chief Examiners, based on the performance of candidates, and on the recommendation of examiners where this is relevant (Writing).
- comparison with statistics from previous years' examination performance and candidature.

A candidate's overall grade is based on the total score gained by the candidate in all four papers. It is not necessary to achieve a satisfactory level in all four papers in order to pass the examination.

Awards

The Awarding Committee deals with all cases presented for special consideration, e.g. temporary disability, unsatisfactory examination conditions, suspected collusion, etc. The committee can decide to ask for scripts to be re-marked, to check results, to change grades, to withhold results, etc. Results may be withheld because of infringement of regulations or because further investigation is needed. Centres are notified if a candidate's results have been scrutinised by the Awarding Committee.

Results

Results are reported as three passing grades (A, B and C) and two failing grades (D and E). Candidates are given statements of results which, in addition to their grades, show a graphical profile of their performance on each paper. These are shown against the scale Exceptional – Good – Borderline – Weak and indicate the candidate's relative performance in each paper. Certificates are issued to passing candidates after the issue of statements of results and there is no limit on the validity of the certificate.

Further information

For more information about BEC or any other UCLES examination write to:
EFL Information
University of Cambridge Local Examinations Syndicate
1 Hills Road
Cambridge
CB1 2EU
United Kingdom

Tel: +44 1223 553355
Fax: +44 1223 460278
email: efl@ucles.org.uk
www.cambridge-efl.org.uk
In some areas, this information can also be obtained from the British Council.

Test 1

READING   1 hour

PART ONE

Questions 1–8

- Look at the statements below and the views on the opposite page expressed by five different people about their careers in retailing.
- Which view (**A, B, C, D** or **E**) does each statement **1–8** refer to?
- For each statement **1–8**, mark one letter (**A, B, C, D** or **E**) on your Answer Sheet.
- You will need to use some of these letters more than once.

Example:

0 I have to meet deadlines in this job.

0	A	B	C	D	E
	☐	■	☐	☐	☐

---

1 The way this market operates has been transformed.

2 New employees are given an overview of how the company works.

3 I've increased my business expertise since joining the company.

4 I enjoy working in retail more than in my former job.

5 Working closely with other people is an important feature of this job.

6 Company training is organised so that all staff share common goals.

7 I need to keep up to date with developments in my field.

8 My business would like to employ only people genuinely committed to a career in retailing.

A CAREER IN RETAILING

Keeping the customer satisfied is central to the retail business. But how much job satisfaction can workers in the retail trade expect?

Five people who work in retailing talk about their careers.

A

Steve Cain is deputy director of trading for a large supermarket. He says, "When I moved into the retail sector I found it offered more tangible achievements and rewards than my previous business consultancy work. The power base has changed in the industry, and it's the retailers who are now driving things forward. Before, buyers waited for the product to come in and negotiated the price with the manufacturers, but now in food retailing, it's the retailers themselves who are developing their own brands and fixing prices, so that makes it an exciting field to work in."

B

Virginia Clement is support and development manager for a large clothing department store. "This means I am responsible for all the buying and merchandising. This demands teamwork, and for me this is one of the most attractive aspects of working at head office. You have a lot of contact with people, from shop floor staff to suppliers. We work in a very open environment and we're very team orientated. Each team is responsible for getting a particular product to the store on time and in the right quantities."

C

Tim Edlund, who works in buying for a large clothing store, says, "The buyer has to have some flair for design, but balancing that, you need a strategic view and business acumen. There are numerous factors influencing a buyer's choice of product range for each season. I have to be aware of current trends in the suppliers' market, competitors' activity and both local and global customer demand. I go all over Britain to keep abreast of this information. Working hours are very irregular, so it's the complete opposite to a 9 to 5 job. It can be extremely exhausting, but I love it."

D

Diane Maxwell is buying controller for women's wear for a home shopping catalogue company. She says that, despite the hard work, her job remains varied and satisfying. "I've gained a huge range of skills with the company in all kinds of fields, both through formal courses and by means of on-the-job training. The scope of the buying role is extremely broad. It's not just about the product. The focus of the job is on producing a profitable range and that requires extensive business knowledge."

E

Jan Shaw is personnel director of a supermarket. She says, "What we really want to do in our company is take on people with a real interest in trade rather than managers who only want to complete a job as fast as possible. Our new graduate recruitment programme aims to do exactly that. The induction programme introduces all aspects of working for our company, giving early responsibility and first-hand experience of the company's working culture. Career development within the company is based on general management skills rather than specialisation, so whatever department they are in, employees will focus on similar aims."

PART TWO

Questions 9–14

- Read this text from an article about job references.
- Choose the best sentence from the opposite page to fill each of the gaps.
- For each gap **9–14**, mark one letter (**A–H**) on your Answer Sheet.
- Do not use any letter more than once.
- There is an example at the beginning, (**0**).

REFERENCES CANNOT ALWAYS BE TRUSTED BY
POTENTIAL EMPLOYERS

'Dull, but reliable, will make a good parent' – so said a head teacher's reference which I was once sent for a school-leaver. (**0**) ....H........

Most references are unreliable, although recruiters usually ask for them. Few ask for character references today, as these have proved useless. (**9**)............... However, these cannot always be trusted. A few may be biased. (**10**)............... This can also occur if there has been friction between boss and subordinate over personal or business matters.

On the other hand, there can also be positive bias. An employer who wants to get rid of someone may fail to mention any relevant failings or even give a glowing report to help the individual go quickly. (**11**)............... But if they do, the law in Britain says they owe a duty of care to both the employer to whom it is supplied and to the individual to whom it refers.

Most written references are unreliable because they are not specific enough. So how do you, and a potential employer, ensure that any reference given on your behalf is genuinely helpful? (**12**)............... Employers normally expect two: one, your immediate superior in your current or most recent job; the other, your boss in the post before, so long as it was in the last five years or so. For a senior post, more may be required.

For their part, no prospective employer should approach your current employer until you have an offer 'subject to references' and you have given permission. (**13**)...............

Once you get the offer, and before giving permission to make contact, tell your boss and explain that the prospective employer will be asking for a reference. Do this face-to-face and during the meeting describe the job for which you have applied. If you can provide a job description or the relevant job advertisements, even better. (**14**)...............

Even if your referee does express some doubts about your fitness for the post, don't worry, employers often prefer to back their own judgement.

Example:

A It would also be wrong for anyone to contact your penultimate firm before then because word may reach your current employer on the grapevine.

B In fact, employers do not have to give references at all.

C These might include your boss's immediate senior and someone at the same level as your boss who is familiar with your work.

D Your boss can then match the reference needs to the needs of the job.

E What they seek are references from previous employers.

F Some managers think it an act of disloyalty if an employee applies for a job elsewhere and will give poor references or only weak praise.

G Firstly, as an employee, make sure you choose the right referees.

H It amused me at the time, but said more about the referee than the candidate.

PART THREE

Questions 15–20

- Read the following article about negotiating and the questions on the opposite page.
- For each question **15–20**, mark one letter (**A**, **B**, **C** or **D**) on your Answer Sheet for the answer you choose.

The ability to negotiate successfully, to reach agreements with other people or parties, is a key skill in any business. This negotiation could be with a buyer or seller and it almost always involves an element of compromise. But, when entering negotiations, you should always keep in mind that it is almost impossible to negotiate and make agreements successfully if you think you can't afford to 'lose' or walk away from what is on offer. This will result in your avoiding asking for anything more than what you think the other side will give without a dispute. You become a passive observer, with the other side dictating the terms.

In most negotiations one side has more to offer than the other and proper planning can help minimise the effects of this imbalance. Decide on set limits for what you can offer before negotiations begin. There are always advantages you can offer the other side, and you clearly have benefits they want or need or they would not be negotiating with you. In fact, the buyer or seller often wants you more than you think, so it is to your advantage to try and see things from their point of view. The better you know their real needs or wants – not just the ones they have told you – the more successful you will be, and the less likely you are to fall into the trap of giving them more than you really need to.

But it is also true that a concession they really need or will value from you won't cost you as much as it benefits them, and yet may still leave you with everything you want. If you know the other side must reach agreement on a deal by a certain date for financial reasons, your willingness to comply with that date could be worth a great deal of money to them, without costing you much, if anything at all. It is up to you to find out what the other side really needs.

Untrained negotiators often allow their feelings to become too involved and they may take each rejection of a proposal as personal rejection. So they become angry with the other person, or blame them for failing to reach an agreement. While it is important to be yourself and, on occasion, not be afraid to express how you honestly feel, it is important to judge carefully when to do this. It is particularly important to maintain a polite and friendly personal relationship when you are facing a difficult negotiation, but keeping negative personal feelings out of negotiation doesn't mean hiding your personality.

Think carefully about your negotiation schedule. Take breaks, particularly during times when you cannot agree over a particular point. But if you have to continue the negotiation on another day, make it soon, and keep the momentum of the negotiations. As long as you are still talking and meeting, you build rapport with the other party; learn more about what they need and ensure that your company is the one most likely to make the deal. This may require both patience and perseverance – but patience pays!

To 'win' a negotiation then, means that neither side should feel that they have 'lost'. You should know what you can offer the other side and know exactly what they want. If you have done everything you can and the deal remains outside the limits you have defined for yourself beforehand, then walk away from it. Either way, you're a winner!

15 What does the writer advise us to remember when we start negotiations?

    A   You should not ask for too much.
    B   You shouldn't feel you have to accept the proposed deal.
    C   It is better not to be too aggressive in negotiations.
    D   You should have many different offers ready.

16 Why does the writer suggest that you put yourself in the other side's position?

    A   because they may have lied about what they want
    B   in order to avoid being trapped into making a deal you cannot change
    C   because it is likely that they have more to offer than you do
    D   in order to be able to see your real value to them

17 The writer says that one advantage of making a concession to the other side is that

    A   you will be able to get something from them in return.
    B   it will please them without any inconvenience to you.
    C   the other party will be more willing to meet deadlines.
    D   you will make more money on the deal.

18 The writer feels that expressing personal feelings

    A   is especially beneficial when negotiations are going badly.
    B   may result in bad decisions being made.
    C   often leads to anger during negotiations.
    D   may be positive at certain times.

19 What advice does the writer give concerning the negotiating schedule?

    A   Use breaks to discover more about the other party's needs.
    B   If serious disagreement occurs, postpone the meeting until another day.
    C   Don't lose the rhythm of the discussions.
    D   Continue the meeting until you reach an agreement.

20 What important piece of general advice is given in the article as a whole?

    A   Find out about the personalities of the people you will be negotiating with.
    B   When negotiating, be prepared to offer more than you originally planned.
    C   You shouldn't worry if negotiations break down.
    D   Do not allow your personality to intrude on negotiations.

PART FOUR

Questions 21–30

- Read the article below about the impact of technology on the environment.
- Choose the best word to fill each gap from **A**, **B**, **C** or **D** on the opposite page.
- For each question **21–30**, mark one letter (**A**, **B**, **C** or **D**) on your Answer Sheet.
- There is an example at the beginning (**0**).

Business and the environment

These days in business, people have to face many challenging questions when . . .(**0**).ᴬ. and implementing new projects in undeveloped areas of the countryside. One issue which has to be faced is whether it is possible to introduce new technology without destroying the local environment.

Economic . . .(**21**). . . and environmental conservation are often seen as natural enemies. It is unfortunate that in the past this has often been true, and it has been necessary to choose between . . .(**22**). . . the project or protecting the environment. However, by taking environmental considerations . . .(**23**). . . at an early stage in a project, companies can significantly reduce any impact on local plants and animals.

For example, in southern Africa, a company called CEL was asked to put up 410 km of a power transmission line without disturbing the rare birds which inhabit that area. The project was carried out with . . .(**24**). . . disturbance last summer. What may surprise many business people is the fact that this consideration for local wildlife did not in any way . . .(**25**). . . down the project. Indeed, the necessary advance planning, . . .(**26**). . . with local knowledge and advanced technology, . . .(**27**). . . that the project was actually completed ahead of schedule. CEL was contracted to finish the job by October and . . .(**28**). . . to do so two months earlier.

CEL is one of those companies which is . . .(**29**). . . to the principle of environmental conservation. Many other companies have yet to be . . .(**30**). . . of the importance of balancing the needs of people with those of the environment. However, it may be the only realistic way forward.

Example:	**0**	**A**	**B**	**C**	**D**
		▬	☐	☐	☐

0   **A**   designing   **B**   conspiring   **C**   drawing   **D**   scheming

21   **A**   development   **B**   progression   **C**   rise   **D**   increase

22   **A**   running   **B**   dealing   **C**   controlling   **D**   leading

23   **A**   deeply   **B**   gravely   **C**   seriously   **D**   severely

24   **A**   bare   **B**   smallest   **C**   least   **D**   minimal

25   **A**   turn   **B**   slow   **C**   speed   **D**   hold

26   **A**   tied   **B**   combined   **C**   added   **D**   related

27   **A**   led   **B**   caused   **C**   resulted   **D**   meant

28   **A**   managed   **B**   succeeded   **C**   achieved   **D**   fulfilled

29   **A**   promised   **B**   persuaded   **C**   convicted   **D**   committed

30   **A**   argued   **B**   convinced   **C**   urged   **D**   impressed

PART FIVE

Questions 31–40

- Read the article below about Newtown.
- For each question **31–40**, write one word in **CAPITAL LETTERS** on your Answer Sheet.
- There is an example at the beginning, (**0**).

Example: | 0 | T | H | E | R | E | | |

Services and utilities in Newtown

In Newtown ....(**0**)......... are: branch offices of 48 banks, more ....(**31**)......... 100 registered legal and commercial law offices, four important insurance companies, and a branch office of the International Business Bank. The telephone service ....(**32**)......... recently been improved by the installation of a new digital system, so businesses will experience ....(**33**)......... difficulty in obtaining telephone lines. The city has excellent resources to meet all travel requirements. Gateway International Airport is within 20 km ....(**34**)......... the centre. The train station has both intercity and local services, and express routes run from the coach station, ...(**35**)......... is not far away. Newtown Business Information Service, located in the centre of the city, offers ....(**36**)......... range of services to match the needs of businesses. Advice on location, recruitment and marketing is available, in addition ....(**37**)......... highly qualified and experienced translators and interpreters. The International Business Exhibition Centre is the largest ....(**38**)......... best equipped in the country. Approximately 50 specialized international trade fairs are held on its premises every year. ....(**39**)......... of the city's greatest advantages is its wide diversity of industry, combining manufacturing with a range of other services. For visitors to Newtown there is a wide choice of hotels, as ....(**40**)......... as numerous restaurants and other facilities.

PART SIX

Questions 41–52

- Read the text below about a management training course.
- In most of the lines **41–52** there is one extra word. It is either grammatically incorrect or does not fit in with the meaning of the text. Some lines, however, are correct.
- If a line is correct, write **CORRECT** on your Answer Sheet.
- If there is an extra word in the line, write **the extra word** in **CAPITAL LETTERS** on your Answer Sheet.
- The exercise begins with two examples (**0**) and (**00**).

Examples:	**0**	C	O	R	R	E	C	T	
	00	T	H	E					

Management Development Programme

0 We are proud to present this Management Development Programme as a five-day

00 opportunity to improve your personal and the interpersonal management skills.

41 Managing – the human side of many enterprise – today calls for top-level talents in

42 self-management and the management of others and this type course offers the inside

43 track to gaining skills which needed to achieve outstanding effectiveness. It is designed

44 for executives at all levels, to strengthen core skills in the areas of management

45 and communication skills. By the end of the course, individuals will have been taken a

46 major step forward in their ability to achieve truly excellent levels of performance

47 from themselves and others. To maintain a high level of stimulation throughout course,

48 a variety of learning methods will be employed. These include formal lectures,

49 team exercises and case studies. All will be carefully managed to ensure you that

50 learning is developed through relating to each one individual's own work experiences.

51 In order to ensure that each participant derives the maximum of benefit from

52 the course, numbers are limited to 15. So don't delay – book your place now!

For more information, please contact the number overleaf.

WRITING   1 hour 10 minutes

PART ONE

Question 1

- The graph below shows the profit or loss made on three new products (A, B and C) in the year following their introduction to the market.
- Using the information from the graph, write a short **report** on changes that occurred between February 2000 and the end of the year.
- Write **120–140** words on a separate sheet.

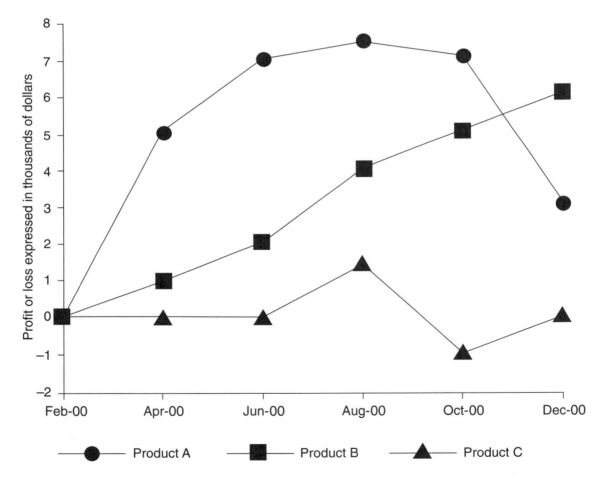

PART TWO

Answer **ONE** of the questions 2, 3, or 4 below.

Question 2

- Your company or organisation is considering the best way to improve efficiency. You have been asked to write a **report** giving recommendations on this.
- Write the **report**, outlining some of the problems the company has concerning efficiency and suggesting solutions. Refer to at least two of the following areas:
  - staffing levels
  - administration
  - communications
  - management
- Write **200–250** words on a separate sheet.

Question 3

- The company you work for faces increasing competition and the managing director has asked you to suggest ways of meeting this challenge.
- Write a **proposal** for the managing director, including the following information:
  - reasons for the increased competition
  - ways to increase sales
  - any extra resources that might be needed
  - any disadvantages there might be.
- Write **200–250** words on a separate sheet.

Question 4

- An international fund is offering grants to small businesses to improve their facilities. Your manager has decided to apply and has asked you to write on behalf of the company.
- Write a **letter**, including the following information:
  - a brief background to your company
  - which facilities a grant would enable you to improve
  - what the future benefits to your company would be.
- Write **200–250** words on a separate sheet.

LISTENING   Approximately 40 minutes (including 10 minutes' transfer time)

PART ONE

Questions 1–12

- You will hear the organiser of an annual conference attended by the sales representatives of a large company. He is telling them about the arrangements for the end of the conference.
- As you listen, for questions **1–12**, complete the notes using up to **three** words or a number.
- After you have listened once, replay the recording.

---

1   The computer session has been moved to Room 110 and the . . . .

. . . . will now be held in Room 201.

2   Team Leaders are to take keys and . . . . to Point B by 3 o'clock.

3   Team Leaders will not have to do any . . . . this afternoon.

4   Airport coaches will leave tomorrow morning from the . . . .

marked *Airport*.

5   Local buses will leave from . . . .

6   Next year's conference will probably be held at the . . . . in

Birmingham.

7   Information about the . . . ., for example, will be sent later.

8   The guest speaker next year will lecture on . . . .

9   This afternoon Alan Smith will speak in Room . . . .

10   Complimentary videos are available from . . . .

11   The video features new . . . .

12   The party is at 8 pm this evening in the . . . .

PART TWO

Questions 13–22

- You will hear five different people who all run their own business. They are talking about how they raised the money to start their business.
- For each extract there are two tasks. For Task One, choose the type of business from the list **A–H**. For Task Two, choose the source of funding for the business from the list **A–H**.
- After you have listened once, replay the recording.

Task One – Type of business

- For questions **13–17**, match the extracts with the types of businesses described, listed **A–H**.
- For each extract, choose the business described.
- Write one letter (**A–H**) next to the number of the extract.

13	**A** a travel agency
	B a supermarket
14	**C** a building firm
	D a clothes manufacturer
15	**E** a fast food outlet
	F a business bookshop
16	**G** a firm of accountants
	H a business language school
17	

Task Two – Source of funding

- For questions **18–22**, match the extracts with the sources of funding, listed **A–H**.
- For each extract, choose the source of funding described.
- Write one letter (**A–H**) next to the number of the extract.

18	**A** a large company
	B a gift of money from a friend
19	**C** sale of shares as a limited company
	D money borrowed from family
20	**E** the sale of the owner's property
	F the investment of the owner's savings
21	**G** state funding
	H a bank loan
22	

PART THREE

Questions 23–30

- You will hear a radio presenter interviewing a businessman called Jim O'Brien.
- For each question **23–30**, mark one letter (**A**, **B** or **C**) for the correct answer.
- After you have listened once, replay the recording.

23 Jim leaves his house early in the morning because

    A   he enjoys driving his car fast.

    B   he wants to avoid the heaviest traffic.

    C   he lives a long way from his office.

24 Jim says that the problem with meetings is that they

    A   always go on for much too long.

    B   are an expensive luxury.

    C   are not as enjoyable as talking informally.

25 Why did Jim lose his previous job?

    A   There were problems with punctuality.

    B   There were disagreements with management.

    C   The company was bought by another company.

26 How did Jim's employment with Hacker begin?

    A   He started a new branch in the UK.

    B   He went to run a branch in the US.

    C   He took over the UK branch.

27 Jim thinks that the perfect worker

    A   has a lot of new ideas.

    B   is young and ambitious.

    C   fits in with the company's methods.

28 Why does Jim have lunch in his office?

    A   He doesn't want a long break.

    B   He likes to eat early.

    C   He doesn't want to meet anyone.

29 What new development is happening in the company this year?

    A   They are focusing on selling through shops.

    B   They are moving into some new offices.

    C   They are making changes in the management.

30 Jim never works late at his office because

A   he wants to spend his evenings entertaining clients.
B   he can take work home with him if necessary.
C   he doesn't like sitting behind a desk to work.

That is the end of the Listening Test. You now have ten minutes to transfer your answers to your Answer Sheet.

SPEAKING   16 minutes

SAMPLE SPEAKING TASKS

PART 1

The interlocutor asks you questions on a number of work-related and non work-related subjects.

PART 2

(The candidate chooses one topic and speaks about it for one minute.)

A Market Research: the importance of doing market research before launching a new product

B Finance: the importance of foreign investment for a company

C Training: how to monitor internal staff training schemes effectively

---

PART 3

For **two** candidates

Customer Involvement

Your company has decided to try to increase customer involvement in the range and quality of its products. You have been asked to consider how this could be done.

Discuss, and decide together:

- how customer opinion of products can be obtained most effectively

- what use a company should make of information provided by customers

---

For **three** candidates

Employee of the Year Award

Your company has decided to introduce an *Employee of the Year* award. You have been given the task of organising this scheme.

Discuss, and decide together:

- what criteria should be used to select the winner

- which people inside and outside the company should be asked to help choose the winner

- what kinds of rewards would be most suitable for the winner

---

Test 2

READING   1 hour

PART ONE

Questions 1–8

- Look at the statements below and at the five short advertisements for MBA (Master in Business Administration) courses on the opposite page.
- Which advertisement (**A**, **B**, **C**, **D** or **E**) does each statement **1–8** refer to?
- For each statement **1–8**, mark one letter (**A**, **B**, **C**, **D** or **E**) on your Answer Sheet.
- You will need to use some of these letters more than once.

Example:

0 This course offers the most competitive prices.

---

1 This course is staffed by well-known tutors.

2 There are facilities for students with disabilities.

3 This course uses a system of continuous assessment.

4 If you study on this course, you must live in the college for several days.

5 Teamwork is essential on this course.

6 You can plan your attendance to fit in with your own requirements.

7 Individual tuition is offered at this institution.

8 Work experience at a senior level is essential for acceptance on this course.

A

> **MBA at Alpha College**
>
> Gain an international business qualification at Alpha College in London.
> Total quality course at a truly competitive price.
> A brighter portfolio means brighter prospects.
>
> Quality output demands quality input; there are therefore minimum requirements for applicants:
> - Education at least to graduate level.
> - Minimum five years' experience at managerial level.
>
> Four ten-week terms (Monday to Thursday): short, highly intensive learning opportunities for the committed businessperson. No weekend or residential school attendance required.
> Contact us direct to hear more. Phone, fax and email numbers overleaf.

B

> **MBA the Harvey Business School way**
>
> Looking for the best? The highest quality does not come cheap. When you consider the calibre of the world-famous professors you will be studying with, you will understand why our course is not the cheapest available. We do, however, offer total flexibility – you can arrange your hours to suit your own pattern of work and personal obligations.
> N.B. Final examinations in June every year.
>
> All our teaching premises are wheelchair accessible.
> For further details call 0207 66718 now, or email us on harvey@interschool.com.uk

C

> **Gain the MBA recognised worldwide**
>
> Unlike other MBAs, the Carfax College MBA is known all over the world and is praised by employers for its realistic approach. The entire course is based on projects and case studies, and progress is monitored and graded throughout the course. You must be willing to work closely with others, as this is an integral part of the learning process. For a brochure, contact the address overleaf.

D

> **Part-time MBA course in Dulwich**
>
> Need to sharpen up your cv? Employers demand the highest qualifications but are rarely willing to release their best employees for long periods of time. The Dulwich MBA therefore offers a three-year part-time course; only day release is necessary, apart from the four-day residential summer school in July or August each year. As the course is spread over three years, there are greater opportunities for assimilation of the information which you acquire. All key texts were published in the last five years.

E

> **Flexibility at Elwood**
>
> Flexibility is vital in today's business world. We therefore offer a modular course, which means that you can gain any of the following qualifications while following the General MBA course:
> - Bachelor of Business Administration (2 years)
> - Certificate or Diploma in Financial Management (2/4 semesters)
> - Diploma in Personnel Development Studies (4 semesters)
>
> It is this type of flexibility, so important throughout business today, together with the vitality of our approach, which makes our course the best on the market. Specially tailored one-to-one or small-group courses for the highly experienced manager also available.
> Call the number overleaf for a free brochure.

PART TWO

Questions 9–14

- Read this text taken from an article about using wind to generate power.
- Choose the best sentence from the opposite page to fill each of the gaps.
- For each gap **9–14**, mark one letter (**A–H**) on your Answer Sheet.
- Do not mark any letter more than once.
- There is an example at the beginning (**0**).

Using wind to generate energy

Using the wind to generate energy is often considered unfeasible. In Great Britain, however, wind power is no longer a subject for cranks and dreamers. (**0**) ....H........ The wind now generates enough electricity to supply 250,000 people. Power companies are investing heavily in the business and windmills are becoming a common sight. (**9**)............... Even though wind power is clean and does not produce any greenhouse gases, pressure groups are determined to prevent its spread.

The National Wind Power Company wants to develop a huge wind farm on the top of Flaight Hill, an extremely beautiful area of Northern England. If they are given the go-ahead, the company will erect 44 rotors there. (**10**)............... They complain that the 60 metre turbines will spoil one of Britain's last remaining areas of natural beauty. They say that this is totally unacceptable. (**11**)............... They say that because the turbines are usually seen from some way away, their size would not be noticed because of the scale of the countryside.

The idea that wind farms ruin rural areas is not accepted by the British Wind Energy Association. The only problem is that people haven't got used to them yet. (**12**)............... They also claim that using the wind is an essential element in attempts to reduce pollution. And this is not all. (**13**)............... To support this, they point to statistics which show that 51 per cent of the power generated by wind turbines can be extracted, compared with about 30 per cent of that generated by coal-fired power stations.

The government is keen to boost the amount of electricity generated by renewable energy sources. In 1994, renewables, including the wind, produced just 2 per cent of Britain's electricity, compared with almost half from coal-powered stations. In future, the government would like to see at least 10 per cent of the nation's power coming from the wind. (**14**)............... This, however, would cover up to 1,250 square miles of countryside. One answer is to locate some of them at sea. It is estimated that as much as 20 per cent of Britain's energy needs could be supplied by offshore wind turbines by the year 2025.

Example:

A Local residents are determined to fight this plan.

B They also dismiss claims that wind technology is inefficient.

C However, this development has not been universally welcomed.

D To achieve this, some 40,000 300-kilowatt turbines would be needed.

E In a press release they state that the countryside is always changing and they deny that wind machines look ugly.

F Recent research, however, has indicated some new problems.

G Such allegations are dismissed out of hand by the company.

H It is now regarded as an important and economically viable source of energy.

PART THREE

Questions 15–20

- Read the following extract from an article about a British businessman and the questions on the opposite page.
- For each question **15–20**, mark one letter (**A**, **B**, **C** or **D**) on your Answer Sheet for the answer you choose.

Gordon Kent is the kind of tough English northerner who runs things his own way. Contrary to what is normal in big corporations today, his company has no remuneration committee, it is short on part-time directors and it has no qualms about employing family members. Mr Kent is chairman and chief executive of the engineering firm William Kent, which has been a family business since the middle of the last century. Until a week ago none of this would have made the headlines. But a rival engineering company has changed this with its £58 million hostile takeover bid, putting Kent's management style in the spotlight. Kent is a fighter: "All my career, I've battled. I've had to battle with customers and suppliers and management."

This will certainly not be his first fight. In 1980, when borrowing money was costing more than 20 per cent, his father was in favour of closing the business. Gordon was not; he forced his father off the board of directors and saved the company. He says, "A difference of views arose. I said the company could either be run by me, or by him, but I couldn't stay there and implement his policy. There was a board meeting and he was persuaded to withdraw."

He says his toughest battle was not taking on his father, but forcing his 160-strong workforce to accept automation at the factory in 1982. "I was really in a difficult position then. The management were against me, the men were against me. The change meant they would have to work a lot harder. I got them all together, and I just said, 'We've got to make this work – it's all our livelihoods at stake.' I was determined to make this business work to save the British steel foundry industry." He won that battle too. Rationalisations, cost-cutting, and a string of 14 acquisitions followed, and the lossmaking family business became a recognised leader in the steel castings industry.

Kent makes running William Kent sound like a military operation, and there is something in his clipped language which is irresistibly reminiscent of the army. His management style is unashamedly autocratic. "I have a very loyal team, and, yes, they have to work hard but they relish it," he says. But unusually for a publicly quoted company, his loyal staff include his wife, Alison, a lawyer who works as a consultant for the company. "I'm not frightened of having to justify this," he says. The shareholders are getting a good deal out of his wife, he reckons, as the company would probably have to pay double for the same services from any other consultant.

Kent robustly defends his own pay and the generous terms of his contract. He reckons he is worth it. "There is a £5 million 'key man' insurance policy on me, and some of our banking arrangements are dependent on me staying with the company. So the outside world reckons I'm fairly important – that isn't just my opinion."

He describes himself as being like the captain of a ship, and he has a firm belief in experience rather than management theory. "You've got to learn your management skills by practical experience; otherwise you confuse delegating with passing the buck and you don't know when people are talking rubbish. I have the strength to fight off this takeover bid. For me it's war. I am autocratic, because that's how you win. When you cut out all the emotion, it's down to money. William Kent is worth much more than this most inferior rival company has suggested. And I know I will be able to convince the shareholders of this."

15 Why is Kent's company in the news?

    A   He has problems with management.
    B   Another company wants to gain control of it.
    C   He is looking for new advisers to help run it.
    D   There have been complaints about his management style.

16 When the company went through a difficult period in the early 1980s, Kent

    A   considered resigning from the company.
    B   thought the company was going to go bankrupt.
    C   made his father give up his power over the company.
    D   persuaded his father to change his policies.

17 Kent says that he introduced automation at his factory because he

    A   wanted to make the future of the steel industry more secure.
    B   thought that his men were not working hard enough.
    C   needed to cut down on the running costs of the company.
    D   believed it would encourage team spirit in his workforce.

18 How does Kent say he feels about having his wife working for the company?

    A   embarrassed that people know about it
    B   certain that she is better than other consultants
    C   afraid that people will misunderstand her role in the company
    D   confident he can defend her contribution to the company

19 With regard to his own position in the company, Kent says

    A   people outside the company think he's overpaid.
    B   if he left, the company would lose some of its bank contracts.
    C   he's the most important member of the company.
    D   the value of his work justifies an increase in his insurance policy.

20 Kent says that his management style is characterised by

    A   being able to persuade shareholders to accept his point of view.
    B   showing no sign of emotion when dealing with financial matters.
    C   proving to his rivals that he is a strong leader.
    D   giving orders and expecting others to obey them.

PART FOUR

Questions 21–30

- Read the article below about the importance of communication in business.
- Choose the best word to fill each gap from **A**, **B**, **C** or **D** on the opposite page.
- For each question **21–30**, mark one letter (**A**, **B**, **C** or **D**) on your Answer Sheet.
- There is an example at the beginning (**0**).

Business communication

One of the most important features in any business is communication. Good communications are required at all . . .(**0**).A. of the business process. Businesses employ, and are owned and run by, various groups of people. Workers, directors and shareholders are three important groups closely . . .(**21**). . . with a business. Other influential groups include customers, suppliers and the government.

Communication . . .(**22**). . . between these groups and the individuals who make up the groups. Within . . .(**23**). . . companies internal communications occur at, and between the various levels. Directors communicate with one another concerning the company's overall strategy. They . . .(**24**). . . managers of their plans, and the managers then communicate with the other employees. . . .(**25**). . . are conducted concerning pay and working conditions. Managers communicate decisions and orders and try to . . .(**26**). . . morale and motivation through good communication. Employees . . .(**27**). . . communicate with each other, for example over production and wages.

External communication occurs when a company's directors or employees communicate with those individuals and groups who . . .(**28**). . . with the company. Shareholders receive copies of the company's annual accounts, together with the . . .(**29**). . . of the Chairman and Directors. Government departments require statistical and financial information from the company. An advertising agency is . . .(**30**). . . about the company's advertising policies. Customers need to know if goods have not been despatched and suppliers contacted if their goods have not been delivered. Reliable and effective communication is one of the key elements which leads to efficient management of a company.

Example:	**0**	A B C D

0   **A** stages   **B** grades   **C** parts   **D** degrees

21   **A** implicated   **B** committed   **C** involved   **D** interested

22   **A** takes place   **B** takes in   **C** takes over   **D** takes hold

23   **A** singular   **B** lone   **C** individual   **D** unique

24   **A** reply   **B** show   **C** acquaint   **D** inform

25   **A** Interrogations   **B** Questions   **C** Negotiations   **D** Interviews

26   **A** grow   **B** mount   **C** gain   **D** improve

27   **A** besides   **B** also   **C** such   **D** like

28   **A** cope   **B** engage   **C** deal   **D** relate

29   **A** files   **B** reports   **C** articles   **D** profits

30   **A** enquired   **B** prepared   **C** consulted   **D** warned

PART FIVE

Questions 31–40

- Read the article below about technical writers.
- For each question **31–40** write one word in **CAPITAL LETTERS** on your Answer Sheet.
- There is an example at the beginning, **(0)**

Example:	0	F	E	W				

Technical writers

Twenty years ago, there were only a ....**(0)**......... technical writers and they were employed to write complicated specifications for computer programmers or aeronautical engineers. These days, ...**(31)**......... is a rapidly expanding profession and technical writers are in great demand. They are now involved ....**(32)**......... producing all kinds of documentation, from the user guides that come with word processing packages ....**(33)**......... sophisticated online tutorials. Surprisingly, it is not always necessary to have ....**(34)**......... strong technical background in order to become a technical writer. However, ...**(35)**......... are certain skills which every technical writer must possess.

Firstly, it is very important to be able to write well. This means ....**(36)**......... only knowing the basics of spelling, grammar and punctuation, but also having the ability to condense and organise complicated information to ....**(37)**......... it simple to understand. A good writer must also be able to cope with meeting tight deadlines.

As far ....**(38)**......... career prospects are concerned, after gaining valuable experience, many technical writers have the opportunity of taking on management roles. They may then ....**(39)**......... responsible for the work of other writers within a particular company, or they may prefer to become contractors. This means selling their services through an agency employing many freelance technical writers, ...**(40)**......... services are charged to companies at an hourly rate.

PART SIX

Questions 41–52

- Read the text below about the life cycle of a product.
- In most of the lines **41–52** there is one extra word. It is either grammatically incorrect or does not fit in with the meaning of the text. Some lines, however, are correct.
- If a line is correct, write **CORRECT** on your Answer Sheet.
- If there is an extra word in the line, write **the extra word** in **CAPITAL LETTERS** on your Answer Sheet.
- The exercise begins with two examples, (**0**) and (**00**).

Examples:	**0**	C	O	R	R	E	C	T	
	00	W	H	E	N				

The product life cycle

0   Products have a limited life, not only from the consumer's viewpoint, but also

00   when as far as the producer is concerned. For example, a particular model

41   of car might last 5 years before production is stopped and it is replaced

42   for by a completely new model. New inventions and technology

43   have to made many products obsolete. Fashion can be another major

44   as influence on the life of a product. Some products survive because

45   they now sell after in different areas. Products, since they have a

46   limited life, all have a life cycle. It is obvious that different products

47   are last for different lengths of time but their life cycles have certain

48   common in elements which can be described as the introduction, growth

49   and maturity stages. The length of the product's life cycle can often be

50   extended by a modifying the product in some way and this is often done by

51   companies to keep their products on the market for a longer period.

52   Provided that the product remains so competitive, this can be much less

     expensive than developing a new model.

WRITING   1 hour 10 minutes

PART ONE

Question 1

- The bar charts below show the results of a survey carried out recently among the directors or senior managers of small and medium-sized businesses.
- Using the information from the bar charts, write a short **report** on these businesses.
- Write about **120–140** words on a separate sheet.

SMALL AND MEDIUM-SIZED BUSINESSES
SURVEY OF DIRECTORS/SENIOR MANAGERS

The numbers above the columns represent the number of answers.

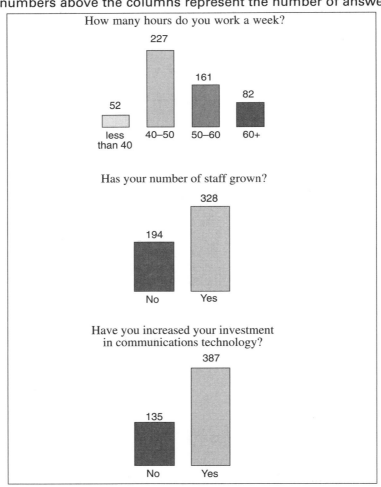

PART TWO

Answer **ONE** of the questions 2, 3 or 4 below.

Question 2

- You recently attended a trade fair in another country. Your manager has now asked you to write a report about your visit to the fair.
- Write the **report**, describing your visit to the trade fair and including the following points:
  - which other companies were represented
  - how you spent your time
  - what information you obtained
  - whether or not you recommend attending the fair next year (and why).
- Write **200–250** words on a separate sheet.

Question 3

- Your Managing Director is concerned to reduce costs and has asked you to make some recommendations on how this might be achieved.
- Write a **proposal** for the Managing Director, including the following information:
  - outlining the areas in which costs could be reduced
  - describing how savings could be made
  - explaining how these changes would affect procedures
  - recommending how to communicate these changes.
- Write **200–250** words on a separate sheet.

Question 4

- You have received the following email from a customer:

> I was surprised to hear a rumour recently that your company is suffering financial difficulties and is likely to go out of business. I'd be very sorry if this were true.
>
> Colin Sanders

- Write a **letter** to the customer, and include the following points:
  - a denial of the rumour
  - a possible reason for the rumour
  - your company's plans for future growth
  - your hope for Mr Sander's continued custom.
- Write **200–250** words on a separate sheet.

LISTENING   Approximately 40 minutes (including 10 minutes' transfer time)

PART ONE

Questions 1–12

- You will hear a presenter on a radio programme giving information about some workshops.
- As you listen, for questions **1–12**, complete the notes using up to **three** words or a number.
- After you have listened once, replay the recording.

CAREER WORKSHOPS

November 7th:

1   Title of workshop . . . .

2   Most suitable for . . . .

3   Seminar on . . . .

4   Location of workshop . . . .

November 14th:

5   Title of workshop . . . .

6   Organised by company called . . . .

7   Applications from . . . . should be sent now.

8   Participants will receive their . . . .

November 23rd:

9   Event organised by . . . .

10   Name of exhibition . . . .

11   Organisers famous for . . . .

12   Information available on suitable . . . .

PART TWO

Questions 13–22

- You will hear five different people talking about advertising campaigns.
- For each extract there are two tasks. For Task One, choose the method of advertising they have chosen from the list **A–H**. For Task Two, choose the purpose of the advertisement from the list **A–H**.
- After you have listened once, replay the recording.

Task One – Method of advertising

- For questions **13–17**, match the extracts with the methods of advertising, listed **A–H**.
- For each extract, choose the method they have chosen.
- Write **one** letter (**A–H**) next to the number of the extract.

13 ....

14 ....

15 ....

16 ....

17 ....

A	television
B	radio
C	national newspaper
D	local newspaper
E	the internet
F	poster
G	direct mail
H	free samples

Task Two – Purpose of advertisement

- For questions **18–22**, match the extracts with the purposes, listed **A–H**.
- For each extract, choose the purpose of the advertisement.
- Write **one** letter (**A–H**) next to the number of the extract.

18 ....

19 ....

20 ....

21 ....

22 ....

A	to advertise a job
B	to launch a new product
C	to announce new opening times
D	to publicise a sale
E	to announce a change in location
F	to change the company's image
G	to give information about sales figures
H	to promote a catalogue

PART THREE

Questions 23–30

- You will hear part of a radio programme in which two businesspeople – a woman called Heather and a man called Alan – are interviewed by a presenter called Sarah.
- For each question **23–30**, mark one letter (**A**, **B** or **C**) for the correct answer.
- After you have listened once, replay the recording.

23 The disadvantage of some business cards is that they

    A   have been produced too cheaply.
    B   include out of date information.
    C   contain too much information.

24 The most important number to include on a business card is your

    A   home telephone.
    B   direct fax.
    C   email.

25 Job titles on business cards

    A   matter less than qualifications.
    B   should always be included.
    C   can be misinterpreted.

26 When choosing a mobile phone, the most important factor is the

    A   message service.
    B   size and weight.
    C   battery life.

27 When you buy a mobile phone, you must

    A   take out an insurance policy.
    B   check the contract carefully.
    C   get an extended guarantee.

28 When packing for a business trip, the most important factor is to

    A   make sure you will always look smart.
    B   know your schedule well.
    C   limit the amount of luggage you take.

29 The biggest problem when travelling internationally on business is

    A   difference of culture.
    B   language barriers.
    C   the time difference.

30 After an important meeting, you should

    A   make notes.
    B   relax.
    C   phone your office.

That is the end of the Listening Test. You now have ten minutes to transfer your answers to your Answer Sheet.

SPEAKING   16 minutes

SAMPLE SPEAKING TASKS

PART 1

The interlocutor asks you questions on a number of work-related and non work-related subjects.

PART 2

(The candidate chooses one topic and speaks about it for one minute.)

A Staff Management: how to achieve and maintain high motivation among a workforce

B Market Research: the importance of carrying out market research for company growth

C Technology: how to plan for the impact of new technology on a company

---

PART 3

For **two** candidates

Cutting Departmental Costs

Costs involved in running your department have recently risen sharply. You have been asked to consider how these costs could be reduced.

Discuss, and decide together:

- what reasons there might be for the sudden increase

- how staff can be encouraged to help reduce costs

For **three** candidates

No-Smoking Policy

Your company is considering introducing a No-Smoking policy. You have been asked to give your opinions on this policy.

Discuss, and decide together:

- what are the advantages and disadvantages of having a No-Smoking policy in a company

- which parts of a company's premises should be included in a No-Smoking policy

- how the company could deal with any objections from staff who are smokers

---

Test 3

READING   1 hour

PART ONE

Questions 1–8

- Look at the statements below and at the reviews of various new business products on the opposite page.
- Which review (**A**, **B**, **C**, **D** or **E**) does each statement **1–8** refer to?
- For each statement **1–8**, mark one letter (**A**, **B**, **C**, **D** or **E**) on your Answer Sheet.
- You will need to use some of these letters more than once.

Example:

0 This product is based on an earlier model.

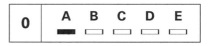

---

1 This product helps you organise your paperwork.

2 This product has a feature that is not essential.

3 It is rather difficult to learn how to use this product.

4 This product is expensive for home use.

5 This product is designed to make your working area look more interesting.

6 Someone from the company can show you how to use this product.

7 This product has a special device for ensuring privacy.

8 This product is not likely to be required by many people.

A

PRINTER

Hamaki UK's new DFG-2000 Bubble Jet printer is ideal for anyone looking to add colour to serious documents and presentations, and is an upgrading of last year's DFG-15. Outstanding graphics make it a leading printer in its class, ideal for a business looking for quality, although its price may put it out of the reach of most private users. The unit can reproduce the finest details and its extended palette of colours means that a wide variety of images can be produced. Operated using software that can spot user errors before they result in poor printing, the machine has a simple two-button control panel. It is also very user-friendly and easy to install.

B

ELECTRONIC MULTIMEDIA BOX

Primal Products is set to liven up even the dullest desktop with its latest range of accessories. Office workers can now express themselves and individualise their working area with the Storage Collection. The Collection is a series of smart-looking boxes for multimedia disks, spoilt only by a rather unnecessary and gimmicky digital display on the front of the box, telling you what disks it contains. Available in bright colours chosen to match hardware trends, the collection is easily carried, which is a definite plus for those who need to take their work home with them.

C

FAX MACHINE

Reak's office machinery further expands its 'Home-office' range of products with the introduction of the RK1 fax machine. To reduce routine filing and save valuable time, the RK1 prints incoming documents and collates them automatically. Its slightly angular appearance is not very eye-pleasing, but it is very inexpensive, can store up to fifty numbers for quick dialling and has a built-in paper cutter.

D

NOTEBOOK COMPUTER

Kipadi, the company responsible for marketing Melon computers, has launched the MH3 notebook computer with unique removable disk drive. This means that each user can keep their own files confidential, on separate disks. The MH3 does take some time to master, and its functions are rather complex. However, it is extremely versatile and is ideal for use in the workplace and at home. It only weighs 3 kg, comes with a one year warranty and is in the mid-price range for notebook computers.

E

PHOTOCOPIER

Peterson's new 'slimline' photocopier is another attempt at making a product as small as possible. It is extremely portable for a photocopier, and even comes with a carrying case. It is very easy to use and includes the offer of a free home or office demonstration if you request one. This is a fairly basic machine, and copy quality leaves something to be desired; however, if you need a portable photocopier this could be for you – although it is difficult to imagine a big market for this type of machine.

PART TWO

Questions 9–14

- Read this text taken from an article on theories of management.
- Choose the best sentence from the opposite page to fill each of the gaps.
- For each gap **9–14**, mark one letter (**A–H**) on your Answer Sheet.
- Do not use any letter more than once.
- There is an example at the beginning (**0**).

Don't follow that theory – think for yourself!

In the 1990s, according to US author Eileen Shapiro, managers have abandoned the right to manage. She argues that managers in the USA have lost confidence. (**0**) ....H........

She describes a corporate culture which is extremely defensive and which has as its motto 'Managers should always follow the latest short-lived management theory, no matter how irrelevant it may be'. (**9**)............... In turn, these have been followed blindly by managers who have given up their central responsibility – taking decisions about their own business in their own particular circumstances.

"I really believe a manager's job is to manage", she says. But increasingly, she feels, they do everything but that. (**10**)............... That's because this, the identification of problems and opportunities, is the scariest part of management. Managers try to avoid the anxiety it brings by simply applying the latest theory to any problem. (**11**)............... Managers should, she believes, confront these head-on.

It is not that Ms Shapiro does not believe in cutting out unnecessary management layers and opening up organisations. Her criticism is that theories are often presented unthinkingly as solutions and are applied by managers who do not really understand what they are saying.

"Theories are often regarded as if they are some sort of miraculous cure for any type of problem", she says. "However, many projects have failed because theories have been applied which were not appropriate to the situation." (**12**)............... The blame for this inappropriate application of theories lies, she claims, mainly at the door of consultancy firms. It is difficult for big firms of consultants to specialise sufficiently. They cannot hope to offer exactly the service that a company requires at a price which the client is able to afford. (**13**)............... This is worse than having no help at all.

One of the most serious potential consequences of following theories without considering whether they are appropriate or not is a loss of staff morale and motivation. Obviously, this is something to be avoided. (**14**)............... However, Ms Shapiro believes that, unfortunately, unless managers begin again to take responsibility for their own actions, that is exactly what will happen.

A They therefore end up developing generalised solutions which are offered to clients regardless of an organisation's specific problems.

B There are many firms of consultants offering help to companies.

C No manager in their right mind would want to work with an angry, cynical or alienated workforce.

D Just because a course of action has succeeded in one context, it does not mean it will be right in other circumstances.

E From 'mission statements' to 're-engineering', she shows how one theory has replaced another in quick succession.

F But in doing so, they often fail to address the real issues.

G They fail to tackle the central management task, which is diagnosis.

H They therefore no longer have the courage or the ability to take responsibility for their decisions.

PART THREE

Questions 15–20

- Read the following article about a successful British businessman and the questions on the opposite page.
- For each question **15–20**, mark one letter (**A, B, C** or **D**) on your Answer Sheet, for the answer you choose.

Every year British universities turn out 15,000 graduates in business studies. Many dream that they will one day be running a major business, wielding power and influencing markets. But only a very few will climb to the top and realise their fantasies. For the rest, compromise, disappointment, mediocrity and an alternative career away from the mainstream action will be their lot. Peter Blackburn is chairman and chief executive of Nestlé UK, which employs more than 12,000 people and has a turnover of £1.8 billion. His advice to those who wish to move ahead of the pack is as straightforward as the man. "Take all your qualifications seriously. Although many top executives do not have first-class honours and it is often a disadvantage to be an intellectual, qualifications are increasingly important, as is the quest for improvement."

"I do feel that an international dimension helps every career. It says something about the person and if they have worked in another language, it gives a manager the important dimension of realising that each market is part of something bigger. Also it is always important in any career to keep your options open as events can take an unexpected turn. When they did for me, I acted accordingly. I still have to pinch myself to remind myself what I am doing. Even 10 years ago I didn't think this is what I would end up having achieved."

"In the end, those that get right to the top retain their 'people touch', which can be very difficult as one gets swept up on the fast track of corporate life. But those who never forget where they have come from and keep their feet on the ground have a real advantage. The important thing is that you should never ask someone else to do something you couldn't do yourself. I am always looking for those who have the determination, the steel to see through our corporate objectives. I also want managers who can be role models for the next generation, people who will be an inspiration."

Blackburn started out working for a small confectionery company and was responsible for clearing up a major financial scandal when it was taken over by a larger company, Rowntrees. This was a project which marked him out and gave him visibility in Rowntrees. While many successful careers can easily be seen as an almost predictable procession, there are always one or two moments when success in a project promotes the executive, bringing star quality and something of an aura. However, if at the decisive moment a mistake is made, then the executive, instead of moving sharply forward, disappears into the pack and others are given their chance.

When Rowntrees was later taken over by Nestlé, Peter Blackburn went on television and argued against the takeover. When the dust settled, the winners rewarded their spirited adversary. "I have always believed in doing the best that I can in any situation. Sometimes you have to make difficult decisions and then it's important to meet them square on. I have been fortunate in that the evolving company that I am now involved with has always believed in strong social values and has behaved as humanely as possible when it has been forced to close or to sell one of its businesses."

Peter Blackburn's career has been marked by two company takeovers. Many successful takeovers have been characterised by the new owners looking at the second layers of management and giving them a free rein. Mr Blackburn has benefited from this process twice and says: "In both the takeovers I have been involved with, success has been achieved because the new owners have not gone in for wholesale clearouts. They have realised that it is the existing people who understand the business and they must be the platform for any growth."

15 Peter Blackburn says that to compete successfully in the job market, people should

    A   be realistic about their abilities.
    B   make sure they choose the right post.
    C   improve their relations with other executives.
    D   have a good educational background.

16 In the second paragraph, Blackburn says his present day achievements are due to

    A   being able to adapt to changing circumstances.
    B   deciding to learn other languages.
    C   having worked for an international company.
    D   staying in the same job for several years.

17 Blackburn says that it's important for a manager to

    A   lead their staff by example.
    B   put ambition above everything else.
    C   demand high standards from their workforce.
    D   move as quickly as possible up the corporate ladder.

18 The writer uses the example of Blackburn's involvement in the Rowntrees Project to show

    A   how problems within a company can be highlighted.
    B   how competitive executives are within a company.
    C   how easily mistakes can be made by executives.
    D   how the management's attention can be drawn to someone.

19 What is Blackburn's attutide towards the company he now works for?

    A   He has some regrets about its public image.
    B   He approves of the way it treats its employees.
    C   He dislikes the demands it makes on him.
    D   He admires the way it explains its decisions.

20 Blackburn attributes the success of the company that have involved him to

    A   the role he played in each of them.
    B   the abilities of the new managers.
    C   the decision not to make radical personnel changes.
    D   the financial support provided by the owners.

PART FOUR

Questions 21–30

- Read the article below about market research.
- Choose the best word to fill each gap from **A**, **B**, **C** or **D** on the opposite page.
- For each question **21–30**, mark one letter (**A**, **B**, **C** or **D**) on your Answer Sheet.
- There is an example at the beginning (**0**).

Market research

Market research has become more and more important in recent years. In some organisations, in fact, managers will not initiate any activity without market research to . . .(**0**).^A. them up.

The first thing to be said about market research is that it is not an . . .(**21**). . . to management decision-making. No form of market research, no matter how deep, complicated and detailed, can ever be seen as a substitute for creative decision-making by professional managers. . . .(**22**). . . its very best, all it can do is . . .(**23**). . . some doubt and clarify the nature of the problem. It may even be seen as a tool which can improve the . . .(**24**). . . of decisions but it is not in itself a decision-making mechanism.

Market research, in . . .(**25**). . . with a number of other approaches in marketing, suffers from the frequent complaint that it is not really accurate. Market research results can never be completely accurate because they . . .(**26**). . . with a dynamic, ever-changing marketplace. It is vital that this is understood by everyone with an interest in the results. There is, therefore, an ongoing need for creativity and imagination when . . .(**27**). . . market research results and when making any . . .(**28**). . . to apply them in the marketplace.

Lastly, it should always be remembered that market research is not an end in itself but simply a . . .(**29**). . . by which some degree of risk can be removed from marketplace activity. If no activity . . .(**30**). . . from the research, then the entire exercise has been completely pointless.

Example:	**0**	**A**	**B**	**C**	**D**
		▬	▭	▭	▭

0   **A** back   **B** follow   **C** keep   **D** lead

21   **A** option   **B** alternative   **C** end   **D** opening

22   **A** For   **B** From   **C** At   **D** With

23   **A** reject   **B** omit   **C** deny   **D** remove

24   **A** quality   **B** goodness   **C** well-being   **D** virtue

25   **A** association   **B** common   **C** addition   **D** connection

26   **A** work   **B** manage   **C** deal   **D** operate

27   **A** deciding   **B** thinking   **C** proving   **D** considering

28   **A** attempt   **B** venture   **C** choice   **D** try

29   **A** mode   **B** means   **C** way   **D** progress

30   **A** shows   **B** produces   **C** results   **D** appears

PART FIVE

Questions 31–40

- Read the article below about telephone skills.
- For each question **31–40** write one word in **CAPITAL LETTERS** on your Answer Sheet.
- There is an example at the beginning, (**0**).

Example: | **0** | I | S | | | | | |

How to deal with difficult people on the phone

One of the skills required of today's successful business people ....(**0**)......... the ability to deal with difficult people on the phone. The Reed Employment agency has come ....(**31**)......... with some advice to help business people get the best from the caller.

First of all, accept that people can be rude when they are ....(**32**)......... pressure. Try to find out ....(**33**)......... they are angry – even if you have to guess. And, importantly, never get angry back. Many problems are caused by a simple misunderstanding. Therefore it is essential ....(**34**)......... remain calm so that you can get to the root of the problem and thus have ....(**35**)......... better chance of resolving it. Understand that maintaining your calm is much easier than it sounds – but you can prepare ....(**36**)......... designing a strategy. Most call centres train staff ....(**37**)......... these techniques; other office workers need to train themselves. The trick is to be really nice back ....(**38**)......... that they end up thanking you for your help, understanding and assistance.

Secondly, listen carefully and empathise with the person making the complaint. You don't ....(**39**)......... to compromise your company or your colleagues just because you show understanding. Agree to a course of action and stick to it and, finally, always try to be courteous. Sometimes you are the one ....(**40**)......... will have to apologise and you just have to accept that.

PART SIX

Questions 41–52

- Read the text below about an international competition.
- In most of the lines **41–52** there is one extra word. It is either grammatically incorrect or does not fit in with the meaning of the text. Some lines, however, are correct.
- If a line is correct, write **CORRECT** on your Answer Sheet.
- It there is an extra word in the line, write **the extra word** in **CAPITAL LETTERS** on your Answer Sheet.
- The exercise begins with two examples (**0**) and (**00**).

Examples:	**0**	I	N						
	00	C	O	R	R	E	C	T	

THE INTERNATIONAL YOUTH SKILLS COMPETITION

0   The International Youth Skills Competition is held in every two years over

00 a period of three days. The purpose is to bring together the world's top

41 young technicians. The standard of work is extremely high and the results are

42 a good indication of a nation's industrial skill base. Teams take their part in

43 a variety of activities ranging from the cookery to leading a hill walking

44 expedition. Naturally, these competitions can be stressful as they test

45 skills to the limit. However, they are also a very marvellous opportunity

46 for young people to learn from one another's performance and develop

47 their own skills. This means that when they return at home they are

48 able to transfer that what they have just practised directly into the

49 workplace. At the end of the competition, the winning contestants who are

50 awarded medals in each event, and the country with the most of medals is

51 declared the overall winner, an honour which is becoming increasingly

52 prestigious as the competition gains our wider recognition throughout the world.

WRITING   1 hour 10 minutes

PART ONE

Question 1

- The bar chart below shows the percentage of sales made by retailers in Britain on each day of a typical week during the years 1996 and 2001.
- Using the information from the bar chart, write a short **report** summarising the changes that took place between 1996 and 2001.
- Write about **120–140** words on a separate sheet.

Day by day: The shoppers' week

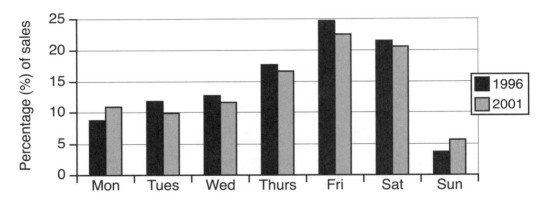

PART TWO

Answer **ONE** of the questions 2, 3, or 4 below.

Question 2

- Your company is considering appointing someone as your assistant. Your boss has asked you to write a short report on whether an assistant would be useful for you.
- Write the **report** for your manager, describing:
  - the advantages to you of having as assistant
  - what difficulties might arise if an assistant is appointed
  - what qualifications and experience would be desirable in an assistant
  - what personal qualities would be desirable in an assistant.
- Write **200–250** words on a separate sheet.

Question 3

- The Marketing Director of the company you work for is keen to improve the way that your company markets its products, and has asked you to propose and improvement.
- Write a **proposal** for the Director, including the following information:
  - reasons for the current method's lack of success
  - your proposal for new method
  - the likely benefits of the new method
  - any possible disadvantages of the new method.
- Write **200–250** words on a separate sheet.

Question 4

- You work for a company producing office furniture and have received a letter from a customer complaining about the non-delivery of two desks.
- Write a **letter** to the customer:
  - apologising for the non-delivery
  - giving reason(s) for the delay
  - offering compensation.
- Write **200–250** words on a separate sheet.

LISTENING   Approximately 40 minutes (including 10 minutes' transfer time)

PART ONE

Questions 1–12

- You will hear the Chairman of the Business Broadcasting Committee of a television company. He is addressing a meeting of the committee.
- As you listen, for questions **1–12**, complete the notes using up to **three** words or a number.
- After you have listened once, replay the recording.

The Chairman's Introduction

1   The meeting was supposed to take place in the . . . .

2   The second point on the agenda concerns the . . . . of

programmes.

3   Fewer people have been watching . . . .

4   More people have been watching . . . .

5   They may need to produce a new programme which will last

for . . . .

The Video

6   The chairman shows a video of a programme called . . . .

7   Business people were not expecting a rise in . . . .

8   Derek Hallam is President of the . . . . Association.

9   Derek Hallam is concerned about the damage to exports caused by a

strong . . . .

10   There is to be a . . . . between AKC and TBN.

11   The price of shares in the chemical companies has risen by . . . .

A Criticism

12   The Institute of Managers has complained about . . . . TV

interviewing styles.

PART TWO

Questions 13–22

- You will hear five different people, who have all been interviewed for jobs with a large international company which is going to build a new factory.
- For each extract there are two tasks. For Task One, choose the job the speaker was interviewed for from the list **A–H**. For Task Two, choose the feeling that each person expresses about changing jobs from the list **A–H**.
- After you have listened once, replay the recording.

Task One – Job

- For questions **13–17**, match the extracts with the people, listed **A–H**.
- For each extract, choose the job each speaker was interviewed for.
- Write one letter (**A–H**) next to the number of the extract.

13	**A**	marketing manager
	B	computer programmer
14	**C**	secretary
	D	personnel management assistant
15	**E**	engineering manager
	F	maintenance supervisor
16	**G**	finance director
	H	quality control manager
17		

Task Two – Feeling

- For questions **18–22**, match the extracts with what people say, listed **A–H**.
- For each extract, choose the feeling expressed.
- Write one letter (**A–H**) next to the number of the extract.

18	**A**	welcomes the opportunity to travel in the new job
19	**B**	is unhappy in his/her present job
	C	considers the new job a promotion
20	**D**	was not happy about their interview
	E	thinks the interview was successful
21	**F**	is undecided about accepting the new job
	G	did not like the new company
22	**H**	would like to live in this area

PART THREE

Questions 23–30

- You will hear part of a radio interview in which a business expert is being asked about consultants.
- For each question **23–30**, mark one letter (**A**, **B** or **C**) for the correct answer.
- After you have listened once, replay the recording.

23 According to Mr Beeston, consultancy is criticised because

    A   it introduces unnecessary changes.

    B   it has become too complicated.

    C   it doesn't always work.

24 He says that the best kind of consultant

    A   makes the company aware of its failings.

    B   works in an equal relationship with the company.

    C   knows solutions and presents them quickly and clearly.

25 What does he say about how the situation has developed recently?

    A   Demand for consultants has increased.

    B   There are more specialised services available.

    C   The cost of consultancy has been reduced.

26 He says that the most successful projects take

    A   many months or years.

    B   at least six months.

    C   as little time as possible.

27 What advice does he give for selecting a consultant?

    A   Decide after several discussions with different consultants.

    B   Make sure the consultant is very knowledgeable.

    C   Choose a consultant who is used to big projects.

28 What difficulty does he explain about the end of a consultancy?

    A   It is hard to apply the recommendations.

    B   The advice which is given is not relevant.

    C   The report is too complicated to understand.

29 He says the best time to use a consultant is

    A   when the tax year starts.
    B   before problems develop.
    C   when profits are reduced.

30 What is his plan for his own future?

    A   to take early retirement
    B   to set up his own company
    C   to write about his experiences

That is the end of the Listening Test. You now have ten minutes to transfer your answers to your Answer Sheet.

SPEAKING   16 minutes

SAMPLE SPEAKING TASKS

PART 1

The interlocutor asks you questions on a number of work-related and non work-related subjects.

PART 2

(The candidate chooses one topic and speaks about it for one minute.)

> **A Technology:** the importance of training staff in how to use new technology when introducing it into the workplace
>
> **B Purchasing:** how to maintain good relationships with suppliers
>
> **C Advertising:** how to achieve a strong visual impact in advertising

PART 3

For **two** candidates

> ### Time Management
>
> Your company has found that ineffective time management is one of the major problem areas throughout the workforce. You have been asked to put forward some suggestions for improving the situation.
>
> Discuss, and decide together:
>
> • why poor time management can become a major problem in companies
>
> • what procedures could be adopted to ensure that time is managed effectively

For **three** candidates

Special Training Course

Your company is considering offering some of its employees the opportunity of attending a special training course abroad. You are a member of the committee which will decide if this plan should be implemented.

Discuss, and decide together:

- what could be the advantages to employees of spending a period of time abroad

- how a company can benefit from this kind of scheme

- how the success of the training course could be evaluated

Test 4

READING   1 hour

PART ONE

Questions 1–8

- Look at the statements below and at five passages taken from a book about famous management thinkers on the opposite page.
- Which passage (**A, B, C, D** or **E**) does each statement **1–8** refer to?
- For each statement **1–8**, mark one letter (**A, B, C, D** or **E**) on your Answer Sheet.
- You will need to use some of the letters more than once.

1 Others in his field think very highly of him.

2 His ideas have spread beyond the business world.

3 He felt that people should be able to enjoy their work.

4 His ideas are more complex than they seem.

5 He did a variety of interesting things before writing his books.

6 His most successful book was written with a colleague.

7 He is particularly skilled at forecasting important developments.

8 Contact with the military was an early influence on his thinking.

A

John Adair

Adair is the pioneering British thinker in the theory of leadership. He was the first person in the UK to hold a professorship in Business Leadership and has published a series of influential books on the subject.

Despite his quiet appearance, Adair has had a colourful life, serving in a Bedouin regiment and working on an Arctic fishing boat! His initial interest in leadership came from his army experience and he used to lecture at the highly prestigious academy where British army officers are trained. He now works as an international consultant.

B

Edward de Bono

De Bono is unusual among major 'gurus' for two reasons: firstly, he was born not in one of the great industrial nations but on the tiny island of Malta. Secondly, his ideas have reached a wider audience than just managers, so that his books have become essential reading in many different disciplines.

Most of de Bono's work has been concerned with the way human beings can train themselves to think more creatively. This apparently simple idea has resulted in 37 books and a highly successful career as a lecturer and consultant.

C

Peter Drucker

Probably no other single thinker has done as much as Drucker to establish management as a serious area of study. Certainly, his fellow management thinkers consider him one of the 'founding fathers' of the discipline, and his books and articles are quoted more than those of any other management writer.

His first book was published as far back as 1939, yet he is still writing and teaching. His greatest distinction has been his ability to predict coming trends in business and economics. As a result, his ideas are treated with the greatest respect and interest.

D

Frederick Herzberg

Although relatively few contemporary management students will have read his books, Herzberg's name is instantly recognisable to anyone who has studied industrial organisations. This is because the American psychologist was responsible for introducing the concept of 'motivation' into management thinking.

As a young man, Herzberg became deeply interested in mental illness and the human need for mental and emotional satisfaction. This led him to criticise the approach of many companies to job design, and to argue for the need for 'job enrichment' to stimulate employees' efforts.

E

Tom Peters

The American's reputation was created in the 1980s by the spectacular success of one book, *In Search of Excellence*, co-written with Robert Waterman. The two were working together as management consultants and no-one expected their first (and only) book to end up selling 5 million copies worldwide!

Although his ideas have been criticised, Peters' popularity as a speaker and writer has continued to grow. So much so that Peters has created his own business to market books, videos and consultancy based on his work.

PART TWO

Questions 9–14

- Read this text taken from an article about health clubs.
- Choose the best sentence from the opposite page to fill each of the gaps.
- For each gap **9–14**, mark one letter (**A–H**) on your Answer Sheet.
- Do not use any letter more than once.
- There is an example at the beginning (**0**).

Travel stress brings boom to health clubs

A rapid growth in business travel has provided a lucrative spin-off for British health clubs as companies try to prevent hard-working executives from suffering travel-related stress. Health clubs are fully booked throughout the coming months all around the country and many are planning to expand their facilities.

(**0**) ....H........ According to Gillie Turner, group marketing manager for the Champneys group of health clubs, during the last recession executives lost many of their extra benefits as companies cut back. (**9**)............... She says that large companies also seem to have decided that it is no good sending someone to a country like Spain as a reward for doing a good job, because they will simply eat too much and flop onto a beach. (**10**)...............

Champneys, the company acknowledged as the market leader in this field, is now planning to introduce a special 'Profiting from Stress' course, which will run over three days. (**11**)............... Jonathon Stapleton, general manager of Champneys, says that modern corporate life being what it is, most business travellers find that they are having to do the work which – even a year ago – was done by two. (**12**)...............

To meet this new demand, other health clubs are also thinking of introducing similar schemes. Clare Brandish, the sales and marketing director of another health club, has noticed a marked change in the clientele at her club. (**13**)...............

Businesses of all kinds are anxious to reduce absenteeism. (**14**)............... Much of the problem is caused by long periods away from home, irregular hours, business entertaining and jet lag.

According to the Guild of Business Travel Agents, sales of business-class airline tickets have risen by 12% in the past year, hotel bookings have gone up by 36% and car hire has risen by 24%. Dave Reynolds, the GBTA chief executive, says that the trouble is that the same number of people are being asked to travel more often. He comments that it is no wonder they need to take a break in a health club.

A It has been calculated that about 40 million working days are lost each year in Britain because of stress, ten times as many as are lost to industrial disputes.

B Instead, they want executives to become fitter so that they can do even more for the company in the future.

C This has involved a considerable rise in the number of business bookings, whereas previously most clients came as private individuals.

D Now they are being restored, as industry realises that the health of its executives is vital.

E But who will benefit most from these developments?

F Because of the pressures this imposes, many companies have now decided that it is worthwhile paying for their senior executives to take a proper break and get advice on how to combat stress.

G Executives taking part in it will be given massages and health treatments, workouts and a range of talks on how to deal with stress, especially when travelling.

H So what's the reason for this new trend?

PART THREE

Questions 15–20

- Read the following article on recruiting and managing staff and the questions on the opposite page.
- For each question **15–20**, mark one letter (**A**, **B**, **C** or **D**) on your Answer Sheet, for the answer you choose.

As a manager in the service industry sector, I've looked at hundreds of CVs in my time. They are not necessarily the bland documents some bosses might think they are! They are full of little pointers towards individuals' personalities and suitability for the job. The first thing I always look at is an applicant's employment record. I check for continuity and stability. If somebody has a long list of previous jobs, all of varying length, alarm bells start ringing. Rather than an irregular route from job to job, what I hope to see is stable career progression. What does their career path look like – is it all steps forward, or are there a lot of sideways moves? And I am always pleased to find a family person with children, because in my experience they tend to be responsible and reliable.

I never rely on CVs alone. We get applicants to fill in one of our own application forms. We ask why they've applied, what their aspirations and personal goals are, and also about their interests and hobbies and any clubs they belong to. That gives you a useful insight into their personality and lifestyle. The application form also enables us to test how much people have actually been progressing in their careers, because we ask for details of the salaries they have received for each job.

It's always worth looking at CVs and designing application forms with great care. Taking on employees might be rewarding, but it is also a big investment for any business. Mistakes in choosing staff can cost companies dear, so it makes sense to spend time ensuring you get the right person.

In the service sector, one of the aims of companies is to maintain and improve customer service, and this is achieved partly through low staff turnover. You need to take on people who understand that, and will want to stay. That's why, when you've taken staff on, the next thing is getting the best out of them.

My management style comes from the days when I took over my first business, an ailing road haulage firm which I was certain I could turn into a profitable company. The first thing is to treat others as you'd like to be treated yourself. As soon as I took over the business, I talked to everybody individually, and looked for ways to make sure their particular skills benefited the company.

I didn't have much experience then of managing people, but above all I always tried to be fair and honest with everyone. As a result, I think the staff knew that and accepted my decisions, even if they didn't agree with them all. Also, bosses must be able to communicate. You also need to create team spirit, and build on the strength of the team. I explained my plans for the company to all the staff, and let them know what I needed from them. The lorry drivers responded brilliantly, and were the key to turning the business round. They understood that we had to develop a professional reputation, and from then on the days of poor quality deliveries were over.

Lastly, I am a great believer in profit-sharing. It takes a team to make a company work, so profits should be shared by all. Job satisfaction is important, but it doesn't pay the rent. Shared profit and bonuses help to strengthen team spirit by giving everyone a common goal that they work towards together.

15 What fact does the writer hope to learn from applicants' CVs?

  A that they have experience of many different jobs
  B that their careers have developed steadily
  C the opinion their employers had of them
  D whether they are married or single

16 The writer says the application form is useful because it

  A reveals something of the applicant's character.
  B gives information about the applicant's family.
  C explains what skills the applicant has for the job.
  D shows how much the applicant wants to earn.

17 According to the writer, why are CVs and application forms so important?

  A Interviewing people is an expensive process.
  B They indicate whether applicants really want the job.
  C They indicate whether applicants are efficient or not.
  D Employing the wrong people can be disastrous.

18 One reason why the writer was successful in her first business was that

  A she was used to dealing with people.
  B she was open with the staff.
  C the business was already doing well when she started.
  D the staff agreed with all her decisions.

19 The writer believes profit-sharing is a good idea because

  A it encourages a competitive spirit.
  B everyone earns the same salary.
  C everyone shares the same aim.
  D it creates job satisfaction.

20 Which would make the best title for this text?

  A Profit-sharing as motivation
  B How I turned a business round
  C People – the key to business success
  D The importance of a well-presented CV

PART FOUR

Questions 21–30

- Read the article below about a method of learning languages aimed at business people.
- Choose the best word to fill each gap from **A**, **B**, **C** or **D** on the opposite page.
- For each question **21–30**, mark one letter (**A**, **B**, **C** or **D**) on your Answer Sheet.
- There is an example at the beginning (**0**).

Language learning for the busy executive

If you've ever been told by your boss to improve your knowledge of a foreign language you'll know that . . .(**0**). C . doesn't come quickly. It generally takes years to learn another language well and constant . . .(**21**). . . to maintain the high standards required for frequent business use. Whether you study in a class, with audiocassettes, computers or on your . . .(**22**). . . , sooner or . . .(**23**). . . every language course finishes and you must decide what to do next if you need a foreign language for your career.

Business Audio Magazines is a new product designed to help you continue language study in a way that fits easily into your busy schedule. Each audiocassette . . .(**24**). . . of an hour-long programme packed with business news, features and interviews in the language of your choice. These cassettes won't teach you how to order meals or ask for directions. It is . . .(**25**). . . that you can do that already. Instead, by giving you an opportunity to hear the language as it's really spoken, they help you to . . .(**26**). . . your vocabulary and improve your ability to use real language relating to, for example, that all-important marketing trip.

The great advantage of using audio magazines is that they . . .(**27**). . . you to perfect your language skills in ways that suit your lifestyle. For example, you can select a topic and listen in your car or hotel when away on business. No other business course is as . . .(**28**). . . . and the unique radio-magazine format is as instructive as it is entertaining. In addition to the audiocassette, this package includes a transcript with a business glossary and a study . . .(**29**). . . . The components are structured so that intermediate and advanced students may use them separately or together, . . .(**30**). . . on their ability.

78

Example:	**0**	A	B	C	D
		☐	☐	▬	☐

0   **A**   gain   **B**   result   **C**   success   **D**   outcome

21   **A**   exercise   **B**   performance   **C**   practice   **D**   operation

22   **A**   self   **B**   individual   **C**   personal   **D**   own

23   **A**   after   **B**   then   **C**   later   **D**   quicker

24   **A**   consists   **B**   includes   **C**   contains   **D**   involves

25   **A**   insisted   **B**   acquired   **C**   asserted   **D**   assumed

26   **A**   prolong   **B**   extend   **C**   spread   **D**   lift

27   **A**   allow   **B**   let   **C**   support   **D**   offer

28   **A**   adjustable   **B**   flexible   **C**   convertible   **D**   variable

29   **A**   addition   **B**   supplement   **C**   extra   **D**   manuscript

30   **A**   according   **B**   depending   **C**   relating   **D**   basing

PART FIVE

Questions 31–40

- Read the article below about meetings.
- For each question **31–40** write one word in **CAPITAL LETTERS** on your Answer Sheet.
- There is an example at the beginning, (**0**).

Example:	0	B	Y					

How to make more of meetings

You should know what ends you want to achieve in a meeting before it starts and prepare for it ....(**0**)......... reading any papers circulated beforehand, and carefully thinking about ....(**31**)......... you want to say. This may sound rather boring, but solid preparation is the key to successful meetings. A great ....(**32**)......... of time and energy can be wasted through simple lack of planning.

The most important issues are not always given the most time in the general running of meetings. People are often unwilling ....(**33**)......... discuss important budgetary matters because they do not fully understand them, but ....(**34**)......... becomes an expert when it comes to discussing the colour of the new curtains, or what type of coffee to buy! The discussion of ....(**35**)......... trivial matters as these, therefore, should be saved until the end of the meeting.

During the meeting it is essential to stick to the agenda so ....(**36**)......... to avoid the common problem of repetition. At the same time you ....(**37**)......... to be sensitive to other people's ideas and feelings, and never lose your temper. Be prepared to accept ....(**38**)......... implement a suggestion that is contrary to ....(**39**)......... own ideas if it is an improvement on them; such honesty and flexibility are signs of good leadership and earn respect.

Finally, remember that when a decision is made it is important to act ....(**40**)......... it and to honour all the commitments you have made in the meeting.

PART SIX

Questions 41–52

- Read the text below about customer care.
- In most of the lines **41–52** there is one extra word. It is either grammatically incorrect or does not fit in with the meaning of the text. Some lines, however, are correct.
- If a line is correct, write **CORRECT** on your Answer Sheet.
- If there is an extra word in the line, write **the extra word** in **CAPITAL LETTERS** on your Answer Sheet.
- The exercise begins with two examples (**0**) and (**00**).

Examples:	**0**	T	H	A	T				
	00	C	O	R	R	E	C	T	

Customer care

0 Apart from ensuring that an efficient electricity supply for our

00 customers, NatElectric provides an invaluable service in other areas

41 as well. While our Customer Helpline (charged at local rates) is the

42 first point of contact with when you want to make an enquiry and

43 we receive a huge number of calls from customers – on

44 average, there are 50 000 calls a one week. Available 24 hours

45 a day, seven days a week, 365 days a year, our Helpline on advisors

46 aim at to answer 95 per cent of all calls within 15 seconds. There

47 are more than 200 advisors, working in around the clock to

48 provide for this service, backed by a further 80 support staff

49 who do handle any necessary paperwork. Although our target

50 is to reply to letters within 10 working days, NatElectric regularly

51 responds within three to four days, and we are especially proud of the

52 very high standards achieved of our customer relations team.

WRITING   1 hour 10 minutes

PART ONE

Question 1

- The bar charts below show the number of complaints made by consumers about different types of products and services in the years 1996 and 2001.
- Using the information from the bar charts, write a short **report** summarising the changes that took place in each sector between 1996 and 2001.
- Write about **120–140** words on a separate sheet.

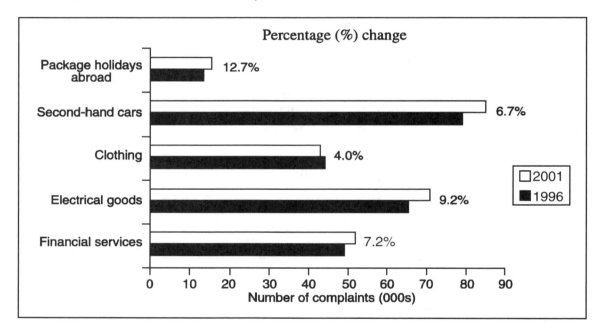

PART TWO

Answer **ONE** of the questions 2, 3, or 4 below.

Question 2

- You have just completed a six-week period working at a different branch of your company. The head of department you normally work for has asked you to prepare a report evaluating the usefulness of the experience.
- Write the **report**, including the following information:
  - what your duties involved
  - the benefits and drawbacks of the experience
  - advice for colleagues preparing for a similar experience.
- Write **200–250** words on a separate sheet.

Question 3

- The Human Resources Director of the company you work for is keen to improve the way in which the company recruits new staff, and has asked you to propose an improvement.
- Write a **proposal** for the Director, including the following information:
  - the problems caused by the current system of recruitment
  - your idea for a new method
  - the likely benefits of the new method
  - any possible disadvantages of the new method.
- Write **200–250** words on a separate sheet.

Question 4

- The company you work for is currently investing heavily in systems to improve the quality of its products.
- Write a **letter** to your key customers explaining:
  - why this decision has been taken
  - what changes will be made within your company
  - how customers will benefit from these changes.
- Write **200–250** words on a separate sheet.

LISTENING Approximately 40 minutes (including 10 minutes' transfer time)

PART ONE

Questions 1–12

- You will hear the General Manager of Artis Ltd giving her staff instructions about the arrangements for a visit to the company by a group of international agents.
- As you listen, for questions **1–12**, complete the notes using up to **three** words or a number.
- After you have listened once, replay the recording.

ARTIS LIMITED

Arrival

Briefing notes for visit of foreign agents

1   The agents will be brought to Artis . . . . at 9 am.

2   The agents will need to be taken to the . . . . by 9.30 am.

Rest of day

3   The first place for the agents to see is the . . . .

4   The second place is the . . . . department.

5   In the cafeteria, a video of the new . . . . will be shown.

6   The last place they will visit will be the . . . .

Must remember

7   All staff must . . . .

8   It's necessary to have two . . . . available at all times.

9   Each agent must be given an . . . . before the presentation.

10   The agent from Bolivia needs an . . . .

Evening entertainment

11   The latest time to arrive at the restaurant is . . . .

12   The . . . . will be at 9 pm.

PART TWO

Questions 13–22

- You will hear five different people talking about a special training programme for their company.
- For each extract there are two tasks. For Task One, choose the person who is speaking from the list **A–H**. For Task Two, choose the opinion that each person expresses from the list **A–H**.
- After you have listened once, replay the recording.

Task One – Person

- For questions **13–17**, match the extracts with the people, listed **A–H**.
- For each extract, choose the person who is speaking.
- Write one letter (**A–H**) next to the number of the extract.

13	....	**A**	the sales director
		B	the managing director
14	....	**C**	a secretary
		D	a new junior manager
15	....	**E**	the advertising manager
		F	the finance director
16	....	**G**	the catering manager
		H	the information technology manager
17	....		

Task Two – Opinion

- For questions **18–22**, match the extracts with what the people say, listed **A–H**.
- For each extract, choose the opinion expressed.
- Write one letter (**A–H**) next to the number of the extract.

18	....	**A**	There are good ideas, but little of practical value.
19	....	**B**	The sessions go on too long.
		C	It may be difficult to remember everything.
20	....	**D**	There are too many specialised sessions.
		E	The eating arrangements should be improved.
21	....	**F**	Technology isn't being given enough importance.
22	....	**G**	The training methods are old-fashioned.
		H	People expect too much from the programme.

PART THREE

Questions 23–30

- You will hear part of a conversation between two company employees, a woman called Rose and a man called Steve.
- For each question **23–30**, mark one letter (**A**, **B** or **C**) for the correct answer.
- After you have listened once, replay the recording.

23 The main benefit of suggestions schemes is that they improve

    A   profitability.
    B   motivation.
    C   efficiency.

24 When receiving a suggestion, it's essential to

    A   publicise it.
    B   implement it.
    C   research it.

25 In this scheme, it will be necessary to exclude

    A   staff in research and development.
    B   junior staff.
    C   senior management.

26 The reward for a successful suggestion will be paid

    A   over a five year period.
    B   after three years.
    C   at a fifth of the total value.

27 When starting the scheme, Rose and Steve will emphasise how it could

    A   increase sales.
    B   be enjoyable.
    C   help promotion.

28 The scheme will be started at

    A   a regional office.
    B   head office.
    C   all offices.

29 Staff will make their suggestions by

   A   using a special box.
   B   sending a memo.
   C   telephoning.

30 Rose and Steve will report to the board on

   A   the quality of suggestions.
   B   the value of suggestions.
   C   the number of suggestions.

That is the end of the Listening Test. You now have ten minutes to transfer your answers to your Answer Sheet.

SPEAKING   16 minutes

SAMPLE SPEAKING TASKS

PART 1

The interlocutor asks you questions on a number of work-related and non work-related subjects.

PART 2

(The candidate chooses one topic and speaks about it for one minute.)

A Career development: the importance of acquiring a range of skills throughout your career

B Customer relations: the importance of customer services in maintaining a company's competitiveness

C Finance: how to ensure effective financial controls in a company

---

PART 3

For **two** candidates

Responding to Competition

Your company has recently begun to lose its share of the market due to competition from a new firm which charges customers less. You have been asked to suggest ways of solving the problem.

Discuss, and decide together:

- how advertising could help the company to deal with competition

- what types of incentives the company could offer to customers

---

For **three** candidates

Job Sharing

Your company is considering introducing a system which enables particular jobs to be shared between two members of staff. You have been asked to advise the company whether this scheme should be introduced.

Discuss, and decide together:

- which types of job this scheme would be suitable for

- what advantages and disadvantages there would be for the company

- which types of people would be most suited to working in this kind of way

---

KEY

Test 1 Reading

Part 1

1 A	2 E	3 D	4 A	5 B	6 E
7 C	8 E				

Part 2

9 E	10 F	11 B	12 G	13 A
14 D				

Part 3

15 B	16 D	17 B	18 D	19 C
20 C				

Part 4

21 A	22 A	23 C	24 D	25 B
26 B	27 D	28 A	29 D	30 B

Part 5

31 than	32 has	33 no/little/less	34 of
35 which	36 a	37 to	38 and
39 one	40 well		

Part 6

41 many	42 type	43 which	44 correct
45 been	46 correct	47 course	
48 correct	49 you	50 one	51 of
52 correct			

Test 1 Listening

Part 1

1 marketing seminar
2 (completed) attendance lists
3 paperwork
4 (collection) point
5 (the) West Gate
6 Central Business School
7 timetable
8 creative management
9 610
10 (the) conference office
11 advertisements
12 Garden Room

Part 2

13 C	14 E	15 H	16 A	17 F
18 D	19 A	20 G	21 H	22 E

Part 3

23 B	24 C	25 C	26 A
27 C	28 A	29 A	30 B

Tapescript

Listening Test One

This is the Business English Certificate Higher Level, Listening Test 1.

PART 1

Part One. Questions 1 to 12.

You will hear the organiser of an annual conference attended by the sales representatives of a large company. He is telling them about the arrangements for the end of the conference.

As you listen, for questions 1 to 12, complete the notes, using up to three words or a number.

After you have listened once, replay the recording.

You have forty-five seconds to read through the notes.

[pause]

Now listen and complete the notes.

[pause]

Man: Ladies and gentlemen. If I could just have your attention for a few moments please. I have a few final notices to give you before we all go into this last session of our conference.

First of all, I'd like to say that this afternoon's computer session has proved to be much more popular than we anticipated, so we're moving this session to Room 110. That's on the first floor. This means that the Marketing Seminar will be moved to Room 201. Room 201 is on the second floor. The times for all sessions are unchanged. I hope that's clear to everyone. Yes?

Next, a notice for Team Leaders. Will you please hand in your keys and your completed attendance lists to reception Point B, where I will collect them. Could you do this at the latest by 15.00. By 3 o'clock, please. There is no paperwork for team leaders to do this afternoon, you'll be pleased to know.

Now, I have to inform you of a last minute change for those flying home. No. Don't worry. Nothing major. You'll still be able to enjoy the party this evening. It's just that the coaches to the airport will now leave tomorrow morning a little later, at 9am sharp, instead of 8.30. And please be at the collection point – that's outside – at least 10 minutes before, so I can check your names. The collection point is marked "Airport". Thank you. The other buses – that's the six coaches for local travel – will leave as arranged ... look at your Fact Sheets ... same times ... same place ... for local destinations, go to the West Gate.

Now, to the future. I have a note from Personnel that the venue for next year is already fixed. It will be in Birmingham, and is most likely to be at the Central Business School. Of course you'll get details of things like the timetable nearer the time. One of the guest speakers will be Dr Lewis Worth. Yes, the famous author from the Los Angeles Institute of Business will be talking about Creative Management. I'm sure we'll all be looking forward to that. Again – details will come to you nearer the time.

Oh, talking of speakers, that reminds me, this afternoon there will be a change of speaker. Alan Smith will substitute for Sue Kennedy, who unfortunately is unwell. Same times, but the room will also change, from 600 to 610.

Well, I'd just like to say ... Oh yes ... one more thing. Don't forget to collect your complimentary video from the conference office. You can drop in there any time throughout the afternoon. It's a preview of our new advertisements. I would draw your attention especially to Film 3. Quite a few surprises. Should be good.

So that's it, I think. It's been a highly successful conference this year – as always. So with my thanks to all concerned for the arrangements and my thanks to you all for contributing, I look forward to meeting you individually tonight at the party ... which starts at 8pm in the Garden Room. And I hope to see you all in Birmingham next year!

[pause]

[*Now listen to the recording again.*]

[pause]

That is the end of Part One. You now have twenty seconds to check your answers.

[pause]

PART 2

Part Two. Questions 13 to 22.

You will hear five different people who all run their own business. They are talking about how they raised the money to start their business.

For each extract there are two tasks. For task one, choose the type of business from the list A–H. For task two, choose the source of funding for the business from the list A–H.

After you have listened once, replay the recording.

You have thirty seconds to read the two lists A to H.

[pause]

Now listen and do the two tasks.

[pause]

Man: I'm a one-man, small business. Very small. It was terrible at first. Nobody wanted to know. Construction's the first thing to be hit when there's a recession. No-one wants new houses, schools, nothing. I just took a chance that if there was no *new* project going on then at least people would want repairs. I tried the banks but I couldn't get any help from them. Nothing. No interest. Must have gone to twenty of them. I'd even done research. Showed them there was a demand for my work. But they're not interested in small firms. Lucky I had a brother and an uncle with a bit of money who were willing to help me out. They lent me enough to get going. Now I'm doing OK.

Woman: I did everything by the book – projections, product research. I did the lot. Then I went round the local offices and noticed there was a niche in my part of town for another take-away. So I decided to go for it. I thought about sandwiches at first but then I knew it had to be hamburgers. What else! 90% of people I talked to said there would be a demand. I didn't have any money so I approached a big company – one of the most famous in the world for this kind of business. I did a business plan and after a lot of work they took me on. I joined the franchise scheme. You know – where you borrow from the big company, use their name and pay them back from your profits. And I must say, it's been very successful, so far. Very hard work, but well worth it.

Man: Well, after a long time teaching I thought – no I *knew* – I needed to move on, do something else, and it had to be a good idea to set up my own operation. You only have to look around Central London to see the demand. Everybody's learning English and more and more business people need it. I had worked in business for a number of years and knew I had the experience to make it work. The one big drawback to the whole plan was that no-one was interested in lending me money. It was hopeless. I wasted so much time going to different banks without success. I was just about to give up when I read about the Government Start-up scheme. If they like your idea they give you money. I was lucky. It's a great success.

Woman: It started as a group of friends getting together and talking about a common problem. The high cost of business trips and the need for a reasonable package. Once people know you are going away on business they think you have unlimited funds for it. And we all knew from our own experience that quite the opposite is true when you work for yourself. So we decided to start something ourselves. Our initial enthusiasm soon disappeared when we tried to raise the money to start, though. We were met with a complete lack of interest. So we put together a good business plan and went knocking on doors. We kept at it. We didn't give up and eventually we found a sympathetic bank manager and they advanced us some money. We're doing pretty well now.

Man: Take the number of MBAs for example. Courses are a real growth industry. And where you have courses you must have textbooks. It's about ten standard texts for a first year Business Diploma alone. I thought it was a market I had to get into and everywhere I went people said I had a good idea. Until I asked for money. Then nothing. Goodbye. I knew it would be difficult but I didn't think it would be impossible. But I

was so determined, I decided to put my house on the market, and I put the money I got from that into the business. It was a huge gamble, and it could have ruined me completely, but it's worked, it's really paid off. I'm opening my second branch next year.

[pause]

[*Now listen to the recording again.*]

[pause]

That is the end of Part Two.

[pause]

PART 3

Part Three. Questions 23 to 30.

You will hear a radio presenter interviewing a businessman called Jim O'Brien.

For each question 23–30 mark one letter, A, B or C for the correct answer.

After you have listened once, replay the recording.

You have forty-five seconds to read through the questions.

[pause]

Now listen and mark A, B or C.

[pause]

Man: Good afternoon. It is time for Face to Face. This week, Sonia Kay talks to Jim O'Brien.

Woman: Jim O'Brien heads the UK division of American PC company Hacker. Mr O'Brien, thank you very much for sparing us a few minutes of your busy schedule.

Man: Hello. It's a pleasure. And please call me Jim.

Woman: Well, Jim, can we start by going through a typical day for you?

Man: I usually get up at around 5am. I drive in from my house to the office in London. I get very frustrated sitting in traffic jams so I leave early to beat the rush. I enjoy driving in, it's nice to get away on my own.

Woman: That's certainly an early start!

Man: Yes, well, at 6.30am, I get into the office. I use the time to get through my post and do the things that are difficult to do during the normal working day because of people wanting to see me. Between the hours of 8 and 9 I take care of any European business which needs doing.

Woman: What a schedule! Do you find it exhausting?

Man: Exhausting, no. But, unfortunately most of my time is spent in meetings now, which doesn't really suit my type of personality. I much prefer the hands-on approach – I would rather be out chatting to people than sitting in the boardroom preparing policies and strategies – but that is a luxury I can't afford.

Woman: Could you tell us how you started with Hacker?

Man: I got into Hacker almost by accident. I was chief executive of a meat trading firm called FMC Harris, which was subject to a hostile take-over. At 9am one morning my boss was fired, and by 9.10am I was out too. I spent eight weeks with no job, a wife and children to support, and a house to pay for. Then I was approached by Hacker to set up a UK branch for them. I was reluctant at first, but after a trip to Hacker's headquarters in the US to discuss it, I was chasing *them*!

Woman: It's a big company. Who do you actually work with on a daily basis?

Man: The rest of the management team arrives at around 9am. I work closely with a team of six, including my PA, Alice Lang. She is an integral part of the management system. I was lucky to find her, as it's almost impossible to find the right person for the job. The ideal employee is someone who is willing to work hard and someone who can adapt to the way we work.

Woman: Uh-huh. Right, so let's get you up to lunch-time. After your early start, you must be ready for lunch quite early, too.

Man: Yes, though the actual time varies from day to day. I try to avoid business lunches because I still have the afternoon ahead to contend with. I don't enjoy lengthy meals. So I usually just have a sandwich in the office with Alice.

Woman: And are there any changes planned for the future?

Man: People ask me if I get frustrated or bored, but the job changes constantly. This year we are moving away from wholesale office sales and more into high street retail sales of home computers. This is new ground for Hacker and presents me with a fresh set of challenges.

Woman: Jim, we hear a lot about people working long hours these days. When do you finish work?

Man: I am not the sort of person who enjoys working late. I try to get home by 7. I won't work late at the office sitting behind the desk because I can do something like that equally well at home. But there's no way to avoid entertaining and meeting people in the evening, so two or three nights a week I stay in town. I try to keep work and the weekend totally divorced. The week's devoted to Hacker, but the weekend is devoted to myself and my family.

Woman: Jim, thank you very much. It's been most interesting, and I'm sure our listeners have learnt a lot.

Man: Thank *you*. I've enjoyed it. And if you need any new computers for your offices . . .

Woman: . . . we know who to call!

[pause]

[*Now listen to the recording again.*]

[pause]

That is the end of Part Three. That is the end of the test.

You now have ten minutes to transfer your answers to your Answer Sheet. Stop here and time ten minutes.

Test 2 Reading

Part 1

1 B	2 B	3 C	4 D	5 C	6 B
7 E	8 A				

Part 2

9 C	10 A	11 G	12 E	13 B
14 D				

Part 3

15 B	16 C	17 A	18 D	19 B
20 D				

Part 4

21 C	22 A	23 C	24 D	25 C
26 D	27 B	28 C	29 B	30 C

Part 5

31 it/this   32 in/with   33 to   34 a
35 there   36 not   37 make
38 as   39 be/become   40 whose

Part 6

41 correct   42 for   43 to   44 as
45 after   46 correct   47 are   48 in
49 correct   50 a   51 correct   52 so

Test 2   Listening

Part 1

1 Decision making
2 senior executives
3 (advance) planning
4 University Research Centre
5 Jobs Worldwide/world wide
6 Careers International
7 recent graduates
8 travel costs
9 English Partnerships
10 Building the Future
11 (their original) designs
12 training programmes

Part 2

| 13 B | 14 G | 15 C | 16 F | 17 A |
| 18 B | 19 D | 20 A | 21 E | 22 F |

Part 3

| 23 C | 24 B | 25 C | 26 A |
| 27 B | 28 A | 29 C | 30 A |

Tapescript

Listening Test Two

*This is the Business English Certificate Higher
Level, Listening Test 2.*

PART 1

Part One. Questions 1 to 12.

*You will hear a presenter on a radio programme
giving information about some workshops.*

*As you listen, for questions 1 to 12, complete the
notes, using up to three words or a number.*

*After you have listened once, replay the
recording.*

*You have forty-five seconds to read through the
notes.*

[pause]

Now listen and complete the notes.

[pause]

Woman: And now, before we say goodbye, three
dates for your diaries. Here's what's happening
in November.

First of all, on November 7th, Ashridge Ltd,
the international centre for management
development, are hosting a one-day workshop.
The workshop is called Decision Making and
will be led by Douglas Bernhardt of the Geneva-
based Freeman Research Group. It is open to
all-comers but is really aimed at senior
executives. It will focus on how to gain that
critical edge needed for faster, smarter decision-
making, and how to exploit advance knowledge
of competitive threats. There will also be a
seminar about advance planning in order to
help executives develop commercial foresight.
The cost for the day's training is £435 and, as
you'd expect for this price, a three-course lunch
is included. Booking details are from Kate
Charlton at their Head Office. The workshop
will be held at the University Research Centre.

Next, on November 14th, there's a seminar
and workshop session at the Manchester
Conference Centre called Jobs Worldwide. This
is the only European recruitment fair to
concentrate on giving young graduates
information on training in multi-lingual,
technical or business skills. This has been set up
by the high-profile European consultancy firm,
Careers International. They have apparently had
a good response so far and they will be closing
the bookings soon so this is a last call for recent
graduates to apply. Participants are offered
reimbursement of their travel costs but not any
overnight accommodation they may require.
Applications must be in by November 3rd and
should be sent to Careers International
headquarters in Manchester. Applicants can also
register their interest through email on
www.hrn.demon.co.uk

Finally, an important event which is taking
place on November the 23rd. English
Partnerships is organising an exhibition in

Birmingham to back up a recruitment drive in the building trade. More than 2,500 new jobs in the building industry are to be created, and the exhibition is called, appropriately enough, 'Building the Future'. At the end of the day, participants attending the exhibition will be able to apply for a selection of jobs in the building trade. English Partnerships are therefore trying to encourage everyone seeking work of this kind to attend. They are well-known in the industry for their original designs, and, to demonstrate this, there will also be photographs of some of their recent projects. If you are interested but don't yet have the right skills, they will also have stands with information on appropriate training programmes. So if you're looking for a job or a change of direction, it's worth going along. Free tickets are available from the English Partnerships office in London, from next Friday.

[pause]

[*Now listen to the recording again.*]

[pause]

That is the end of Part One. You now have twenty seconds to check your answers.

[pause]

PART 2

Part Two. Questions 13 to 22.

You will hear five different people talking about advertising campaigns.

For each extract there are two tasks. For Task One, for each question 13 to 17, choose the method of advertising they have chosen from the list A–H. For Task Two, for each question 18 to 22, choose the purpose of the advertisement from the list A–H.

After you have listened once, replay the recording.

You have thirty seconds to read the two lists A to H.

[pause]

Now listen and do the two tasks.

[pause]

Woman: I think it's the best way to do it because it's better to start small rather than spend all that money on TV ads. We could use local stations as well as bigger ones. A lot of young people listen to them regularly and that's the market we want to reach. Also, if we do that, we would be able to get some initial feedback on sales, whether it's selling well or not in the first few months, and then we can decide if we want to make any adjustments before we spend the big money. Bill said he only wanted this to be an experiment at a few branches. If it really goes well, we can have a national campaign when we bring out the rest of the range.

Man: It's so difficult to know the best way to let people know about this, because if you use something that's just visual, you've then got to make a decision about where to put it. And it may get lost in a mass of other advertising. The only way we can be sure that all potential customers are informed is by delivering a leaflet straight to their homes. There'll be plenty of really good bargains to attract them and we could have some extra reductions on the first day just to get things off to a good start. We might be able to get some local celebrity to open it on the first day, but we also need to think how we're going to attract customers for the whole two weeks it's on.

Woman: Listen, I was talking to Anna and she thinks it's the sort of thing that we can get a good response to locally but I really don't agree, so I'm afraid I've overruled her on this. Also, if we use something local, it'll just appear in the classified section and we want a more up-market, boxed ad., and we need to reach the whole country. I know the rates are much higher but we can choose the one we want to get the maximum response possible. Anyway, I think anyone with the right track record for a position like this would only be looking in the more up-market dailies. If it was something we were trying to fill in one of the local branches, it would be a different matter, but for head office we need to attract the best.

Man: As it really only affects people in that area, I think advertising nationally would be a waste of money. It would be much better to take some prime sites at various points along the motorway. We can have them put up about four weeks before the big move. It'll cost less and it's a way of appealing directly to our customers. The thing is, we don't want our regular customers heading off to the old store and then being informed halfway there that it's not there any more. We could lose a lot of business! They need to know well in advance where they've got to go.

Woman: Oh, I don't think it's worth using something like a sports event because you still only get a limited audience. We need to attract a national audience. I'm not even sure we should use local channels because their viewing figures are so small and we need millions of people to see this. I definitely think we've got to go for maximum exposure. It'll be a better return for our money in the end. Also it'll give us a chance to let people know what we really do, rather than just relying on them recognising the logo. People just assume we only do one thing at the moment. We need to build up public awareness of how big our company is. We've got to emphasise how diverse we are and get ourselves recognised everywhere.

[pause]

[*Now listen to the recording again.*]

[pause]

That is the end of Part Two.

[pause]

PART 3

Part Three. Questions 23 to 30.

You will hear part of a radio programme in which two businesspeople – a woman called Heather and a man called Alan – are interviewed by a presenter called Sarah.

For each question 23–30 mark one letter, A, B or C, for the correct answer.

After you have listened once, replay the recording.

You have forty-five seconds to read through the questions.

[pause]

Now listen and mark A, B or C.

[pause]

Woman: Welcome once again to Business Tips, our regular advice slot. Now on today's programme our regular advisers, Heather and

Alan, who both have extensive experience in the demanding world of business, are going to be taking us through some more of those vital tips for business. That means those apparently small details that can make all the difference to your chances of success. Heather, Alan – welcome back.

Man/Woman: Hello, Sarah.

Woman: Now what are you going to start with this week?

Woman: Business cards. We think they're exactly that kind of apparently small detail where if you're not careful you can go dreadfully wrong. It's not just a way of giving your name and address, it's a whole statement of your company's image – it says a lot.

Man: Absolutely. Yeah, one classic mistake people make is trying to cram all manner of details of themselves and their company on to one little card.

Woman: Yeah, for me, it's all about having simple, clear design. It doesn't matter how much you spend, that's the important thing.

Woman: I agree – the crucial things are good design and a strictly limited amount of relevant information.

Man: And these days we all have so many numbers! Office number, home phone, fax, email ...

Woman: *Home* phone?

Man: Yes, really, some people do –

Woman: I'd just go for the fax –

Man: – as long as it's direct. And job titles is another tricky one. Some people love them, others just want to know what qualifications you have. It depends on who you're dealing with.

Woman: Don't forget, too, that they mean different things in different places. Even a title like Vice President can mean someone very senior in one country –

Man: – and nothing very special in another, so they can lead to confusion.

Woman: Right. Now everyone seems to be using mobile phones – any points you'd like to make about them?

Woman: Oh yes, Sarah – you need to choose your phone very carefully. People are usually obsessed about all the wrong things –

Man: – colour, weight, how long the battery's going to last, has it got a nice case ...

Woman: – when what they should be looking at is the service offered. For example, how easily and cheaply can you retrieve your calls, get your messages –

Man: – because that can make all the difference. And there's the paperwork, too.

Woman: You mean the guarantee?

Woman: Well that's always included these days, I think, like the insurance certificate.

Man: But make sure you read through the contract, see exactly what is and isn't included. That's just common sense, really.

Woman: Right, now travel is increasingly part of business life, isn't it, and I wonder if you have some ideas for us there?

Woman: Well, the thing is you need to pay particular attention to your appearance on a business trip so my advice is always take more clothes than you need –

Man: – you never know what's going to happen –

Woman: – then if your trip's extended, you've still got what you need.

Woman: A lot of people think travelling is very glamorous, don't they?

Woman: Yes, but it's hard, too. Of course, it is exciting to experience different cultures –

Man: Even if the language differences can be –

Woman: ... a bit of a problem for some of us! Yes! Tiredness, I think, is the real problem, because the flights can be long, and then you arrive, and you think it's evening, but actually it's only lunchtime there, so you're out –

Woman: Out of sequence?

Woman: Yes. And you've got to stay alert, be efficient. For example, when the crucial meeting's over, you just want to relax –

Man: – but you can't. You've got to sit down and write down the main points, get it down while it's still fresh in your mind.

Woman: And then phone your office?

Woman: Well that depends. It may be night there anyway ...

[pause]

[*Now listen to the recording again.*]

[pause]

That is the end of Part Three. That is the end of the test.

You now have ten minutes to transfer your answers to your Answer Sheet. Stop here and time ten minutes.

Test 3   Reading

Part 1

1 C   2 B   3 D   4 A   5 B   6 E
7 D   8 E

Part 2

9 E   10 G   11 F   12 D   13 A
14 C

Part 3

15 D   16 A   17 A   18 D   19 B
20 C

Part 4

21 B   22 C   23 D   24 A   25 B
26 C   27 D   28 A   29 B   30 C

Part 5

31 up/through   32 under   33 why
34 to   35 a   36 by   37 in   38 so
39 have/need   40 who/that

Part 6

41 correct   42 their   43 the   44 correct
45 very   46 correct   47 at   48 that
49 who   50 of   51 correct   52 our

Test 3   Listening

Part 1

1 Blue Room
2 content
3 (the) Financial World
4 Company Update
5 50 minutes
6 Business Agenda
7 interest rates
8 Small Business
9 domestic currency
10 merger
11 10%/ten per cent
12 aggressive

Part 2

13 D   14 G   15 A   16 C   17 H
18 C   19 F   20 A   21 H   22 E

Part 3

23 C	24 B	25 B	26 C
27 A	28 A	29 B	30 C

Tapescript

Listening Test Three

This is the Business English Certificate Higher Level, Listening Test 3.

PART 1

Part One. Questions 1 to 12.

You will hear the Chairman of the Business Broadcasting Committee of a television company. He is addressing a meeting of the committee.

As you listen, for questions 1 to 12, complete the notes, using up to three words or a number.

After you have listened once, replay the recording.

You have forty-five seconds to read through the notes.

[pause]

Now listen and complete the notes.

[pause]

Man: Right, I'd like to call this meeting of the Business Broadcasting Committee to order. Thank you. This is the first meeting of the new season and we have a great deal to discuss. First I'd like to apologise for the confusion over the meeting room. It *was* to have been the Blue Room, but we've had to use this one – the Red Room because of ... well, I'll spare you the details. Let's get on. Charles, you'll be taking the minutes, as agreed. Right. Meeting commencing at 10am ... or rather 10.04am, to be precise.

This is a strategy and ideas meeting to decide on our programme requirements for the forthcoming TV schedules. We have to discuss ... firstly, if any change is required in the present number of business programmes in the company's output and secondly, the content of these business programmes. These are the only points on the agenda in front of you, but I'm afraid it could be a lengthy meeting.

First. Numbers of programmes. It has been proposed to cancel "The Financial World" or at least the programme in its present format. This programme has been losing audience share for some time. Fewer people are watching it compared to its rival "Company Update" on Channel 7. A major problem with "The Financial World" seems to be its time slot. At present it goes out at 6pm on a Sunday whereas "Company Update" (which used to be broadcast on Sunday) has changed to Monday at 7pm with a repeat at 7am the next morning.

So. Shall we cancel or change "The Financial World"? And if we cancel it what shall we replace it with? A cancellation will leave us with a 50 minute slot to fill with a new business programme.

Now, content of programmes. As an introduction and to get you thinking I'd like you to watch this video. It's the first few minutes of last week's "Business Agenda" TV programme. Take notes and think about content. Ready?

[The Chairperson switches on a video. Music. Voice of a woman TV presenter.]

Woman: "Welcome to another edition of your weekly programme which looks at the latest business events. "Business Agenda"

The business world is still surprised at the latest rise in interest rates announced by the Central Bank yesterday. A full 1% was totally unexpected. To discuss this we'll be talking to the Chairman of the Bank and Derek Hallam, the President of the Small Business Association. Now Derek has been in the news lately. As you may recall, he made a speech to the CBI in which he expressed his concern at the damage being done to exports by the strength of the domestic currency.

We'll be returning to that story later – but first, the other main news story. The proposed merger between the two giant chemical companies AKC and TBN is to go ahead despite objections lodged with the Monopolies Commission. Shares in the companies have increased by 10% since the announcement. A spokesman for AKC has ...

[Return to previous speaker at the meeting]

Man: Right I'll stop it there, but before we begin I'd just like to draw your attention to some negative comments we've had from members of the public, concerning the format of the programme; and secondly, from the Institute of

Managers about aggressive interviewing styles. The details are in the file in front of you. Now to continue ... *(fade)*

[pause]

[*Now listen to the recording again.*]

[pause]

That is the end of Part One. You now have twenty seconds to check your answers.

[pause]

PART 2

Part Two. Questions 13 to 22.

You will hear five different people, who have all been interviewed for jobs with a large international company which is going to build a new factory.

For each extract there are two tasks. For task one, choose the job the speaker was interviewed for from the list A–H. For task two, choose the feeling that each person expresses about changing jobs from the list A–H.

After you have listened once, replay the recording.

You have thirty seconds to read the two lists A to H.

[pause]

Now listen and do the two tasks.

[pause]

Man: This is a great opportunity and just what this region needs. The unemployment here's been very bad and we've been very lucky to be chosen for this new factory. And this position would be a step-up for me ... a real advancement, so to speak. It could lead to me having my own department one day and a senior position. Especially if I pass the certificate in Human Resources which I've almost finished. If I'm appointed, I'd have to draw up a list of everyone who's applied to the company and then help with the selection process. It helps knowing the area and I've already got quite a few contacts and I told them that all of my experience has been working with people.

Woman: I didn't apply for this job. They wrote and asked *me* to come for an informal interview. It must have been because I've had considerable experience with the accounting system they use and I've done a lot of work on pricing and costing of new lines, at quite a high level. They'd like me to start very soon. It's important to be in at the beginning when you deal with the money side, to make sure everyone stays within the budget constraints which you decide. But I'm not really sure about it at all. I've got a good job now and I'm happy where I am and not really looking for a change. It needs a lot of thought as they *are* a good company and ... well I've got the weekend ahead to think about everything.

Man: Yes I know a lot about this company. They are very good and I've had contact with them before, at various trade shows and advertising conferences in this country. It would be good to work for them. I *would* be doing the same sort of thing, except on a bigger scale. It's not a promotion or anything. The same grade and money but ... more presentations and a lot of consumer research. Although I like my present job, this would give me a chance to get around a bit more, to visit their overseas offices. In fact they are launching a big campaign soon in ten different countries and they'd like me to co-ordinate some of it. It would be a great chance and I'd certainly accept it.

Woman: It's going to be a successful venture. I can feel it and I'd really like to be involved. But I expect there were a lot of very well qualified applicants, what with all the word processing courses around and the number of computers in people's homes. But I've got all the keyboard skills, I'm fast and accurate and I can spell well. I've been doing the job for over ten years, since the days of typewriters. This is the same job but I think it would be interesting ... and I like the area. I'd really enjoy living here. Well, you can only hope. You never can tell with interviews.

Man: Yes, indeed. I was very impressed and I must say that ... well perhaps it's best not to say anything. But I do feel confident about it. There were some interesting questions, but my line of work is very technical so you know it or you don't. It's not as simple as people think. It's not just a question of checking the product at the end of a conveyor belt but setting up a continuous system which monitors every aspect of the production process. This is the only way to get an end product without fault. I hope I get the job.

Key

[pause]

[*Now listen to the recording again.*]

[pause]

That is the end of Part Two.

[pause]

PART 3

Part Three. Questions 23 to 30.

You will hear part of a radio interview in which a business expert is being asked about consultants.

For each question 23–30 mark one letter, A, B or C for the correct answer.

After you have listened once, replay the recording.

You have forty-five seconds to read through the questions.

[pause]

Now listen and mark A, B or C.

[pause]

Woman: Hello! I'm very pleased to welcome into the studio today Maurice Beeston, the managing director of Laurel Consulting and an expert in the field of business consultancy. I'm sure many of you will be keen to hear his ideas in this important but difficult area. Mr Beeston, thank you very much indeed for sparing us a few moments of your valuable time.

Man: Thank you. Actually, it's a pleasure to be here. I feel that consultancy is a very misunderstood area, and I'm always glad of any opportunity to shed a little light on it.

Woman: Why do you think it's misunderstood? In what ways?

Man: Well, when consultants are good, they develop a company's capabilities. But when they're bad, they collaborate with bad managers and actually block change. Some promise great success, but there's no way you can ensure that will happen every time. So the end result can be that a situation arises in which the profession starts to get a bad name.

Woman: I see. So what would be good practice – the ideal consultant?

Man: Mmm ... I think there are basically three ...

three *main* types or kinds of consultant. The first type is the expert, and their approach is straightforward: "I know the answer; you don't; pay me some money and I will tell you." The second type is the process consultant who says, "I know nothing; you know everything and I will help you to exploit that." Now, these are both all right in their way, but it's the third way which actually works best, and that's the consulting partnership which says, "You know a lot and so do I; it's not easy but let's work together on solving the problems."

Woman: And is it normally easy to find a consultant who takes an approach you like?

Man: Not always. Mind you, in recent years, we've seen a lot more agencies coming up. This means you have a lot more choice. The agencies are focusing more on specific areas, they're offering more tailor-made services. They haven't got any cheaper, but what they offer is more relevant.

Woman: So that's good news?

Man: Yes, very much so – and it's to everyone's benefit.

Woman: Now, how long would you say a consultancy lasts?

Man: How long is a piece of string? Some consultancy projects take many months and may even stretch into years. But these are rarities. Mostly a consultancy project will last anything up to six months. It could take days or weeks. Good consultants leave their clients as early as possible to ensure that the client does not become dependent on the consultant.

Woman: Right. And how can you choose, identify a good consultant?

Man: It's not easy. Don't just buy big projects. There is the temptation for executives to believe that consultants hold the answers to all known problems. Call them in and they will sort it out. Instead, it's important to know what you want and talk to a number of firms to see which best fits your needs.

Woman: What's the end result, the outcome of the project?

Man: Yes, well, good question – that's what it's all about, isn't it? The problem that many people complain about is that they are left with this huge, long report which takes days to read through. And at the end of it there's lots of super, relevant advice, but the issue is how do you actually put that into practice, how do you make that theory work?

Woman: How do we know when we need a consultant?

Man: Most companies get consultants in at the wrong time. What you should really do is think ahead a bit. But most people are looking at their tax figures or their falling profits and so on. In other words they wait for trouble and then start calling consultants, when they ought to get them before.

Woman: Mr Beeston –

Man: Maurice

Woman: Maurice, it's been extremely interesting talking to you. Can I just ask finally about your own plans for the future?

Man: I think I want to start getting things down on paper, especially after all these years of talking! I'm not thinking about stopping work, that's for sure. People say why not set up your own business – but I'm too old for all that now. I want now to take some time to reflect, to record the ideas and some of the things that have happened to me during my years of working in this field.

[pause]

[*Now listen to the recording again.*]

[pause]

That is the end of Part Three. That is the end of the test.

You now have ten minutes to transfer your answers to your Answer Sheet. Stop here and time ten minutes.

Test 4   Reading

Part 1

1 C   2 B   3 D   4 B   5 A   6 E
7 C   8 A

Part 2

9 D   10 B   11 G   12 F   13 C
14 A

Part 3

15 B   16 A   17 D   18 B   19 C
20 C

Part 4

21 C   22 D   23 C   24 A   25 D
26 B   27 A   28 B   29 B   30 B

Part 5

31 what/anything/everything/all
32 deal/amount   33 to
34 everyone/everybody   35 such   36 as
37 need/have/ought   38 and   39 your
40 upon/on

Part 6

41 while   42 with   43 correct   44 one
45 on   46 at   47 in   48 for   49 do
50 correct   51 correct   52 achieved

Test 4   Listening

Part 1

1 in (3) taxis/by taxi
2 boardroom/board room
3 computer centre
4 quality control
5 TV advert
6 production line
7 clear/tidy their desks
8 mobile phones
9 information pack/info pack
10 interpreter
11 7.30 p.m./half past seven
12 director's speech

Part 2

13 H   14 C   15 D   16 G   17 B
18 C   19 A   20 D   21 H   22 F

Part 3

23 B   24 A   25 A   26 C
27 B   28 A   29 B   30 C

Tapescript

Listening Test Four

This is the Business English Certificate Higher Level, Listening Test 4.

PART 1

Part One. Questions 1 to 12.

You will hear the General Manager of Artis Ltd. giving her staff instructions about the arrangements for a visit to the company by a group of international agents.

As you listen, for questions 1 to 12, complete the notes, using up to three words or a number.

After you have listened once, replay the recording.

You have forty-five seconds to read through the notes.

[pause]

Now listen and complete the notes.

Woman: Right, if that's everyone ... oh, hello Mr Pandon, if you'd sit just there ... right. Now, as I'm sure you all appreciate, it's absolutely vital that the visit goes off smoothly. Most of the agents already do good business with us, but there are several who don't, and I'm very keen to secure contact with them. It could open up crucial new markets.

   I'll go through the day in order. So, they'll be coming here by taxi – I'm expecting three vehicles, at least that's what I ordered. They should be here by 9. We need to allow for delays, and so on, but you need to make sure that you get them to the boardroom before half past, otherwise the whole day will start late. OK, well, after the introductory presentation there, their first port of call's going to be the computer centre. It's the most up-to-date in the region, and should make a good impression. After that we'll take them to see the quality control division. By then, they'll have been on their feet for quite a while, so it'll be over to the cafeteria for refreshments and a showing of the new TV advert on video. Hopefully, they'll be impressed by the image we're putting out. That'll take us to the question and answer session, then lunch. Finally, with all that in mind, they'll be taken down the production line. I think it'll be helpful for them to see our products being assembled.

   Now, there are certain things we must bear in mind during the day. We have to give a really professional impression, so everybody's got to tidy their desks. I don't want any mess at all. We're going to need two mobile phones to hand throughout the day. The second one is just in case the first one stops working or runs out of battery time. Information packs – they're still being printed up, but they'll be ready tonight. All the agents need to be handed their info packs before the start of the presentation. Language – well, it shouldn't be a problem, except for Mr Gonzalez from Bolivia. He must have the interpreter with him throughout the day. He does speak some English, but it's far from perfect, and we don't want him missing important points, or just generally feeling left out. Latin America's a very exciting market at the moment, and I want us to be right in there.

   Now, on to the evening. Well, the booking's made, and it's all arranged, including Ms Winner's special dietary requirements. We've got the private function room at the back, which is very comfortable and should fit us all in nicely. Although the food won't be served until 8 o'clock, there are drinks and so on, so I want everyone there by half past seven. OK? The last point: the Director's speech will be at 9, so be ready for that – he doesn't want to talk to a lot of people who've got their mouths full! Well, I think that's about all ...

[pause]

[*Now listen to the recording again.*]

[pause]

That is the end of Part One. You now have twenty seconds to check your answers.

[pause]

PART 2

Part Two. Questions 13 to 22.

You will hear five different people talking about a special training programme for their company.

For each extract there are two tasks. For Task One, for each question 13 to 17, choose the person who is speaking from the list A–H. For Task Two, for each question 18 to 22, choose the opinion that each person expresses from the list A–H.

After you have listened once, replay the recording.

You have thirty seconds to read the two lists A to H.

[pause]

Now listen and do the two tasks.

[pause]

Woman: Well, it's quite interesting isn't it – I mean, overall ... You're never going to please everyone always. I think one of the main benefits is perhaps something we weren't really expecting – or, at least, *I* wasn't. And that's the way people with different roles, different jobs, are working together here. Sure, my responsibilities do go across the departments – everyone wants a PC, needs help with the software, I'm always hearing about the problems – never good things, of course, with the network... but here we're *sharing* experiences, different viewpoints, bringing in ideas which reflect our different roles. Then again, that's maybe a problem in itself, 'cos I really don't see how I'm going to hold all this in my head. I'm sure that next week, it'll all have disappeared from my memory.

Man: Frankly, I wonder if my time wouldn't have been better spent back in the office. Well – I don't want to sound negative. Oh, maybe it's just me. I grant you, there's some great theories going round. Amazing ideas, really. All these visions of what could really be happening, pictures of the possible future and what have you. But at the end of the day, we'll be back in the same old office, and I'll be typing and running around and still be expected to do ten things at once. So, if I'm honest, I'm not really sure how all these fine speeches are really going to help me in *my* job. A letter's still a letter, isn't it? Mind you, I'm not saying it's not inspirational in some ways.

Woman: I feel very privileged ... and, on top of everything, it's a great way to meet everyone. It's really helping my confidence. The sessions on technology have been interesting, because I know so little about it. They've told me I'll get more on that as time goes by. And, actually, my problem's not really that. Because, well, what *I* need at this early stage is some kind of overview, some kind of feeling of the whole picture ... you know, how it all fits together. I don't know where I'll be in 5 years' time, you see, so I'm not quite sure what I need to know now. And that's why it's a bit frustrating that each lecture seems so separate, so single-issue. I'd like a wider range to be covered.

Man: It's going pretty smoothly, I'd say, all in all.

We've had worse, and we've had better. And given that we had to put the whole menu together at pretty short notice ... Having said that, though, I'm not at all sure *they* see it like that. I don't know, I think half the problem is people come to something like this with so much hope ... I mean, they assume the world is going to change overnight. And, of course, nothing's that simple. I hear them complaining, but not about the food – I'm happy to say! – that it's not quite what they want. Too general, too specific ... and so on. Anyway, the snacks and the lunches seem to have gone down all right, and I suppose that's all I need to worry about!

Woman: Mmm, yes, I think it's been worth it – *is* worth it. It's difficult, of course, balancing the costs and benefits, the time lost from the office, compared to what I'm investing in. But I've always said our staff, our *people*, are our biggest asset, so anything that brings my people up must be of value in itself. Of course, much will depend on the performance reports, which I hope the different departments can draw up for me reasonably soon. Otherwise, I won't really be in a position to know if I did make the right choice. My main reservation at this stage is that I don't see sufficient input on the system, on the IT side of things. And that's a great pity, because it's vital that we exploit our existing computers to get the best out of them. I want a company that's right up to date.

[pause]

[*Now listen to the recording again.*]

[pause]

That is the end of Part Two.

[pause]

PART 3

Part Three. Questions 23 to 30.

You will hear part of a conversation between two company employees, a woman called Rose and a man called Steve.

For each question 23–30 mark one letter, A, B or C for the correct answer.

After you have listened once, replay the recording.

You have forty-five seconds to read through the questions.

[pause]

Now listen and mark A, B or C.

[pause]

Man: Well, I definitely agree with you, Rose, that the suggestions scheme is a good idea –

Woman: Good.

Man: – and it's got the MD's support, which is crucial, of course.

Woman: Yes. Well, I am pleased, because where I've seen these schemes in other companies, they do seem to be valuable, you know, worth setting up.

Man: I suppose because they push profits up?

Woman: Yuh, well, not exactly. I mean, yes, ultimately, that can happen … but it's more that if you get an efficient scheme going, one that runs well, then the real advantage is people feel more involved, that they matter more, so you get more energy around the place.

Man: I see what you mean. OK, so when we get the suggestions in, how do we start? I guess we check out viability – if it's worth going ahead?

Woman: Certainly you've got to be seen to respond. But actually the first thing, crucially, is to acknowledge it. I'd have thought we could use the noticeboard for that, put the suggestions on it, so people see immediately that it goes somewhere.

Man: Right. And now, is there anyone who can't be involved, do you think? I was thinking that the assistants maybe shouldn't –

Woman: Oh no, they should have a say, some of their ideas could be useful, and it's important for them to feel more involved. I was wondering about the directors and so on, because there's a danger –

Man: That their ideas would seem like orders?

Woman: Absolutely. Mind you, I think we can set the thing up so that all ideas are to be judged as ideas, regardless of the level they've come from.

Man: OK – but I do think, whatever level they're at, that I'm not sure about including the Research and Development people.

Woman: I think you've got a point there, yes, I mean R & D could be setting their own agenda because they could just end up putting forward existing ideas, and then getting extra for them.

Man: Yes – we'd have to make sure that that can't

happen. Right, so how should we do the rewards? I was thinking of a proportion of the benefit, once we know it – I mean, assuming the idea runs.

Woman: Oh yes, obviously only the ones put into action will get … so, er, well, it'll depend on when we can see the benefits come in, I suppose, say two years would – or we could pay out over a three year time-scale?

Man: I don't think we can predict the time, it depends on too many factors. Why don't we just say we estimate the value of the idea in terms of worth to the company, and pay a proportion of that right away?

Woman: So, a fifth, for example?

Man: Sounds reasonable. And we work out the time-scale later …

Woman: What matters now, I think, is to get the idea over to people that it's something they'd have fun doing.

Man: More chance of promotion!

Woman: But we can't make any promises there. I'm not even that keen on profit or sales margins here, just the idea that they'll feel good if they come up with new ideas. But then we really don't know exactly where it's going to lead us. It might really vary from office to office.

Man: Mmm … let's start with head office, shall we? Or one of the regions?

Woman: Well, we've got to start somewhere. How about the south-western branch office?

Man: Uh-huh. And then spread to everywhere else later.

Woman: Right. Now, how are they going to get their suggestions to us?

Man: However they want.

Woman: What, even by phone?

Man: Oh, I see what you mean, could be pretty disruptive –

Woman: If we get a lot … or memos –

Man: Would be good. They're simple, direct … in a box, maybe, in Reception –

Woman: But then we'd be putting off any people who don't go in there –

Man: True. OK, they can send them to us then. Well, I hope this is going to work!

Woman: Bound to. It's not a question of whether it works, but how well! We'll need to evaluate it, of course, for the board. They'll want to know how much money we think we're saving.

Man: But I don't think we'll know that exactly for some time yet.

Woman: The same's true for quality issues, too.

Man: Hmm. We could just give an initial report on how many ideas we receive in the first month, or something like that.

Woman: That's the most realistic aim, and it should be enough to start with.

[pause]

[*Now listen to the recording again.*]

[pause]

That is the end of Part Three. That is the end of the test.

You now have ten minutes to transfer your answers to your Answer Sheet. Stop here and time ten minutes.

INTERLOCUTOR FRAMES

To facilitate practice for the Speaking test, the script followed by the interlocutor for Parts 2 and 3 appear below. They should be used in conjunction with Test 1–4 Speaking tasks.

Interlocutor frames are not included for Part 1, in which the interlocutor asks the candidates questions directly rather than asking them to perform tasks.

PART 2: Individual long turn (about 6 minutes)

Interlocutor:
- Now, in this part of the test, I'm going to give each of you a choice of three different topics. I'd like you to select one of your topics and talk about it for about *one* minute. You'll have around a minute to make notes, if you want to.
- All right? Here are your topics. You can make notes on the spare paper while you are preparing to talk. Please don't write anything on your topic card.

[Interlocutor hands each candidate a different topic card each, e.g. Set 1 and Set 5, and some spare paper and a pencil for notes. Candidates have 1 minute's preparation time. Both candidates prepare their talks at the same time, separately.]

Interlocutor:
- All right. Now, *B, would you begin by telling us which topic you've chosen, please?
- When you've finished talking, *A will ask you a question about your talk. *A, you're allowed to take notes while *B is talking.

*B, would you like to begin?

[Candidate B speaks for 1 minute.]

Interlocutor:
- Thank you. Now, *A, is there anything you'd like to ask *B

[A asks a question.]

- Thank you. Now, *A, it's your turn. When you've finished talking, *B will ask you a question about your talk. *B you're allowed to take notes while *A is talking.
- All right? *A, do you need a few seconds to think about your topic again?

[A is allowed 10 seconds if necessary.]

- Can you tell us which topic you've chosen to talk about, *A? Would you like to begin?

[A speaks for 1 minute.]

- Thank you. *B, is there anything you would like to ask *A?

[B asks a question.]

- Thank you.

[Materials are collected.]

*USE CANDIDATES' NAMES THROUGHOUT THE TEST

PART 3 : Collaborative task and discussion (about 7 minutes)

- Now this part of the test is a discussion activity.

[Interlocutor points to the card showing the task while giving the instructions below.]

- You have about 30 seconds to read this task carefully, and then about 3 minutes to discuss and decide about it together. You're expected to give reasons for your decisions and opinions. You don't need to write anything. Is that clear?

[Interlocutor places the card in front of the candidates.]

- Are you ready to begin? I'll just listen and then ask you to stop after about 3 minutes. Please speak so that we can hear you.

[Candidates have about 3 minutes to complete the task.]

[Materials are collected.]

[The Interlocutor asks one or more of the following questions as appropriate, to extend the discussion.]

Example:
- How important is it for companies to consider the wishes of their customers? (Why?)
- Are there any disadvantages for companies in taking into consideration customers' opinions? (Why?)
- How can companies influence customer needs?

- Does advertising have a mainly positive or negative effect on consumers? (Why?)
- Is customer opinion likely to increase or decrease in importance with the growth of Internet trading? (Why?)

- Thank you. That is the end of the speaking test.

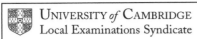
UNIVERSITY *of* CAMBRIDGE
Local Examinations Syndicate

H I G H E R

BEC Higher Reading Answer Sheet

Instructions
Use a PENCIL (B or HB).
Rub out any answer you wish to change with an eraser.

For **Parts 1 to 4:**
Mark one box for each answer.
For example:
If you think C is the right answer to the question,
mark your answer sheet like this:

0	A	B	C̶

For **Parts 5 and 6:**
Write your answer clearly in CAPITAL LETTERS.
Write one letter in each box.

For example: | 0 | E N G L I S H | | |

Part 1

1	A	B	C	D	E
2	A	B	C	D	E
3	A	B	C	D	E
4	A	B	C	D	E
5	A	B	C	D	E
6	A	B	C	D	E
7	A	B	C	D	E
8	A	B	C	D	E

Part 2

9	A	B	C	D	E	F	G	H
10	A	B	C	D	E	F	G	H
11	A	B	C	D	E	F	G	H
12	A	B	C	D	E	F	G	H
13	A	B	C	D	E	F	G	H
14	A	B	C	D	E	F	G	H

Part 3

15	A	B	C	D
16	A	B	C	D
17	A	B	C	D
18	A	B	C	D
19	A	B	C	D
20	A	B	C	D

Part 4

21	A	B	C	D
22	A	B	C	D
23	A	B	C	D
24	A	B	C	D
25	A	B	C	D
26	A	B	C	D
27	A	B	C	D
28	A	B	C	D
29	A	B	C	D
30	A	B	C	D

Turn over for Parts 5 and 6 ▶

108

Part 5

31		1 31 0
32		1 32 0
33		1 33 0
34		1 34 0
35		1 35 0
36		1 36 0
37		1 37 0
38		1 38 0
39		1 39 0
40		1 40 0

Part 6

41		1 41 0
42		1 42 0
43		1 43 0
44		1 44 0
45		1 45 0
46		1 46 0
47		1 47 0
48		1 48 0
49		1 49 0
50		1 50 0
51		1 51 0
52		1 52 0

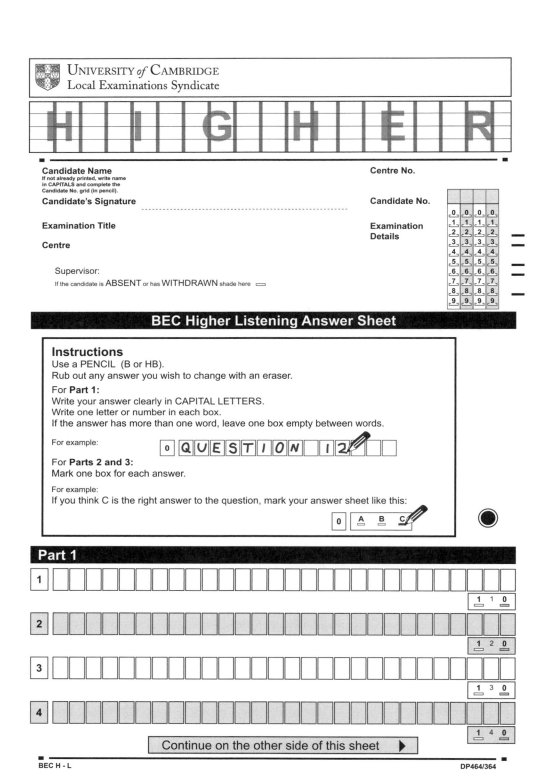

5 ⬚⬚⬚⬚⬚⬚⬚⬚⬚⬚⬚⬚⬚⬚⬚⬚⬚⬚⬚⬚⬚⬚⬚⬚⬚⬚

1 5 0

6 ⬚⬚⬚⬚⬚⬚⬚⬚⬚⬚⬚⬚⬚⬚⬚⬚⬚⬚⬚⬚⬚⬚⬚⬚⬚⬚

1 6 0

7 ⬚⬚⬚⬚⬚⬚⬚⬚⬚⬚⬚⬚⬚⬚⬚⬚⬚⬚⬚⬚⬚⬚⬚⬚⬚⬚

1 7 0

8 ⬚⬚⬚⬚⬚⬚⬚⬚⬚⬚⬚⬚⬚⬚⬚⬚⬚⬚⬚⬚⬚⬚⬚⬚⬚⬚

1 8 0

9 ⬚⬚⬚⬚⬚⬚⬚⬚⬚⬚⬚⬚⬚⬚⬚⬚⬚⬚⬚⬚⬚⬚⬚⬚⬚⬚

1 9 0

10 ⬚⬚⬚⬚⬚⬚⬚⬚⬚⬚⬚⬚⬚⬚⬚⬚⬚⬚⬚⬚⬚⬚⬚⬚⬚⬚

1 10 0

11 ⬚⬚⬚⬚⬚⬚⬚⬚⬚⬚⬚⬚⬚⬚⬚⬚⬚⬚⬚⬚⬚⬚⬚⬚⬚⬚

1 11 0

12 ⬚⬚⬚⬚⬚⬚⬚⬚⬚⬚⬚⬚⬚⬚⬚⬚⬚⬚⬚⬚⬚⬚⬚⬚⬚⬚

1 12 0

Part 2 - Task One

13	A	B	C	D	E	F	G	H
14	A	B	C	D	E	F	G	H
15	A	B	C	D	E	F	G	H
16	A	B	C	D	E	F	G	H
17	A	B	C	D	E	F	G	H

Part 2 - Task Two

18	A	B	C	D	E	F	G	H
19	A	B	C	D	E	F	G	H
20	A	B	C	D	E	F	G	H
21	A	B	C	D	E	F	G	H
22	A	B	C	D	E	F	G	H

Part 3

23	A	B	C
24	A	B	C
25	A	B	C
26	A	B	C
27	A	B	C
28	A	B	C
29	A	B	C
30	A	B	C